Getting Aligned

For

The Planetary Transformation

Your Guide to What's Going on, Why, and your Responsibility

by Tom Price

Getting Aligned

For

The Planetary Transformation

Your Guide to What's Going on, Why, and your Responsibility

Copyright © 2016
Silvercreek Co Publishing, LLC

Silvercreek Co. Publishing, LLC
ThePlanetDailyNews@gmail.com
Salem, Oregon USA
503-951-4167

ISBN-10: 1537514075
ISBN-13: 978-1537514079

Graphics Credits:
  Cover Design by Tom Price
  Sacred Geometry, Line Art, Consciousness Grid © Tom Price
Shutterstock
  World from Space © ixpert
  Gears inside Grandfather Clock © Vivid Pixels

Request for Materials & Presentations

Request for presentations, interviews, editorial permissions, color presentation slides, hard-cover color spiral bound copies, etc., should be addressed to the publisher. See prior page for contact info. Check website (ThePlanetDailyNews.com) periodically, as items may be available for purchase there.

Dedication/Preface

This book effort is dedicated to my mother, Katie Theresa Cox of Southport, North Carolina. This is Andy Griffith's fictional town of Mayberry. She raised eight children alone - - while her husband was away at sea as a merchant marine. Jesus was her man, and as a child I witnessed checks showing up in our mailbox for nearly the exact amount of money for which she prayed. This would be for pressing extraneous expenses such as new eyeglasses or dental work.

Likewise, I recognize my high school history teacher, Mr. Randall - - a quiet, structured person who would not harm a fly. A tiny school with all twelve grades and only sixty in my graduating class (no one dared to do anything out of the ordinary for fear of local gossip), he surprised us one day saying "You gotta read this book". I don't read books. I devoured this one, and read it over and over. It was the "Biography of Edgar Cayce". It talked of the eight dimensions of our existence. This very much impressed me, just like the mailbox incidents above, and my life immediately became a quest to find the common denominator between the "mailbox" and these dimensions.

The book you are reading now is the product of that quest. Apart from the book "Chariots of the Gods", not much happened for twenty years as I got my engineering career squared away, along with marriage and my first child. She was born with turned-in-feet, and after getting frustrated with western doctors, I turned to alternative healing: I literally opened up the Yellow Pages and went to the local "Dandelion Tea and Herb" store. Thus began an amazing thirty-year trek of discovery (starting 1986), which brings me to the Now. Incidentally, my daughter's foot issue was simply that she was still in the fetal position and not quite ready yet to unfold into this new world.

Among the few other books I've devoured, I had my own global business with employees. Being the lone man at the top, I learned to optimize my own "mailbox" and considered writing such self-help books. I'd pretty much woven all the pieces together of how the universe works when, just after 2012, the final pieces literally arrived in my mailbox.

Although I don't read many books, I do write. That's my gift - - being intuitive. During the writing, I made several publishable discoveries, and here they are now in your mailbox. The "2012 Transition" is upon us. This book is your guide to a successful transition. Best of luck!

Keep Updated
On This "2012 Transition"

Visit our **Web Page**

ThePlanetDailyNews.com

for the most immediate updates and products to help you.

Subscribe to **YouTube Channel**

The Positive Side of 2012

For much deeper insights and lessons on 2012
This is a great place to send your friends

FACEBOOK & TWITTER.

Are other avenues to be reminded of new videos
The latest info & up-to-minute news & events
Facebook.com/PositiveSideof2012
Twitter.com/ThePlanetDailyN

Table of Contents

Part I: Sacred Geometry

Part II: History

Part III:
The Melchizedek Files

Part IV: Getting Aligned

Welcome

-Introduction-

Now that "December 21st 2012" has passed, and no Hollywood-based cataclysms have occurred, we can get down to the real business of it all - - the morning after. Exactly like the annual winter solstice on December 21 marks the shortest day of the year, it also marks the beginning of the days getting longer and brighter. It marks a new beginning.

This particular new beginning is unlike any our world, much less our universe, has ever seen. That's the reason Jesus came, and he came to perform a single specific critical task - - which, incidentally, is not mentioned in the Bible.

But there's far more to this new beginning, and that's because its roots go way back in time, well before Jesus. Jesus is a big piece, but nonetheless a piece, of a much bigger plan.

These lectures reveal that much bigger plan, and how it involves the grossly misunderstood history of mankind here on Earth. All the pieces to the puzzle to "What's really going on?" are finally put together in this non-religious package.

"Something" is indeed going on, and we are all active participants.

It's all about the math.

If you think of our universe as a grandfather clock with lots of chimes and cuckoos, then the Flower of Life is the basic mechanical geometry (a simple shape) upon which everything in that clock is based.

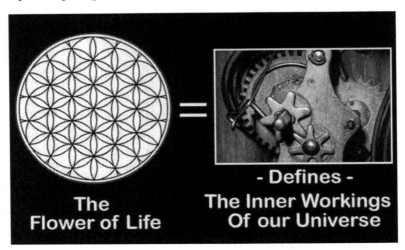

Thus, briefly stated, the Flower of Life is everything. It explains everything. It explains Genesis. It explains our past. It explains why Jesus came, and a whole lot more - - right up to the events happening today.

The Flower of Life is therefore a good and friendly (non-confrontational) lens through which to view our history and situation. That's precisely what we do. The first couple of chapters introduce you to The Flower of Life itself. The subsequent chapters are then our past, present, and (most importantly) our future, with the Flower of Life as our guide.

———

Jesus taught via a "female" approach, and for a very good reason. This, too, relates to the Flower of Life. You will learn what this means, and why Jesus chose this approach. You will also learn there is a "male" approach to what he was teaching.

Many people, and that very much includes me, could not relate to the Bible and Jesus (as much as our parents wanted us to) as a kid. It turns out we probably needed a more "male" approach. We wanted to ignore all the religious fervor and mythology, and get down to the pure grass-roots facts of the matter, i.e., what the heck happened, and what's really going on? You will get those answers. You'll also learn that Jesus was here, and helping us, long before his birth in Bethlehem.

One of my favorite expressions is "Ships are safe inside the harbor, but is that what ships are for?" In these lectures, you are definitely going leave that traditional harbor and sail around. Jesus came here to encourage us to think outside our box, and that (briefly stating all his teachings) "Love is the way home".

When people have near death experiences or essentially anything that really shakes up their life (and they come back a different person with a new outlook on life), aren't these same two premises their hallmarks? They were definitely outside their comfort zone, and suddenly family and love are the only things that count in their lives. Materialism is no longer relevant. These people were more or less shocked into thinking outside their box and learning that Love is the way home.

Wouldn't it be nice if Jesus were here now to talk and use his body language? Even better would be to read his mind and know exactly what he is feeling and thinking. You don't need a language then. You just need to be "tuned in". In a sense, that's what happens to these people with the above near death experiences. They quickly got "tuned in", not to Jesus, but to "Love is the way home" - - i.e., what Jesus taught.

There's another way to get "tuned in". Indigenous people do that today. For example, during special ceremonies an elder may raise his arm and the wind responds by blowing through the trees. In other cases, an eagle may simply levitate overhead, absolutely still, for a few minutes. You will read about such in this book. These individuals are able to communicate directly with the animals and Mother Earth. This means the animals and Mother Earth are communicating as well - - and communicating with each other.

The Great Fall that occurred to us, and Jesus intended to help us recover from, resulted in us losing that ability. Once repairs are made to our species' problem, much like repairing a car or machine, then Love, once again, is the answer. Then we are all "tuned in". There won't be any secrets as we'll know each others thoughts. Also, just like the plants, animals, and Mother Earth, we won't need books or libraries as our true history will be a part of that ongoing connection.

These lectures turned out to be the story of that "Love" connection: How we lost it, the remarkable effort to get it back, how and when do we get it back, and what is required from you as a participant. The latter is what "Getting Aligned" is all about. That story starts eons before Jesus, and is not the symbolic stuff in the Bible. It's a real story with real characters and real decisions that had to be made along the way. It's a fascinating story. That is what's in these lectures.

Finally realize that I wrote this. The information is from the most reliable of sources. Those sources and I have done our very best to provide accurate information, yet that's limited by our interpretation and the actual words used to communicate. Ultimately the burden is on you to pursue these topics on your own, and that is my sincere hope.

With this in mind, fasten your seat belts, and let's get started on this fascinating journey.

- Getting Aligned -
For the Planetary Transformation

Part I: Sacred Geometry

- CHAPTERS -

Getting the answer is not the key....
The key is asking the right question.

Albert Einstein

Chapter 1

-The Energy of the Universe-

The Flower of Life is found in the Bible, in Egypt, and in virtually every culture. It's in the Sumerian records, which are 6,000 years old and are the oldest writings on Earth. The mountains of western Tibet are the home of the largest known pyramid in the world [1]. A beautiful white pyramid with a solid-crystal capstone, a glacier hides it except for a few weeks per year. There are no drawings or inscriptions anywhere to be found inside. However, on one ceiling was the only artwork - - The Flower of Life.

Here is the Flower of Life as it is most commonly shown in these ancient pyramids, etc.

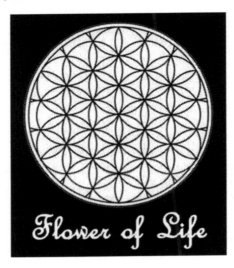

Flower of Life

The Flower of Life does not explain why we are here, but rather it explains *how* we are here. To better understand this, pretend that our universe is a big grandfather clock. The outer face of that clock (which is the clock face itself, all the other clock faces, and all the bells and whistles) is the universe as you and I see it.

Think of the Flower of Life as the inner mechanism of that clock. This means that the Flower of Life is very dynamic. It's being used at every moment of your life to keep everything running smoothly. However, it's important to realize that it runs on energy. Everything does. Thus we need to first discuss energy, and get you comfortable with that. That is the subject of this current chapter.

1.1 *The Energy of the Universe*

Pythagoras, Plato, and many others of ancient Greece thought that the universe consisted of six basic ingredients or elements. These are Earth, Air, Fire, Water, the Great Void, and the Ether (See Figure next page).

The world of chemistry was unknown; the atom was unknown; the concept of energy was unknown. Yet, they knew there was something, not unlike what we know as energy today, and they called it the Ether. Today it is more commonly called the Prana.

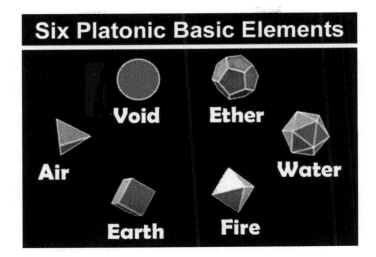

Spiritual people, both then and now, refer to this mysterious Prana as the Life-Force. They insist that there is the Great Void, and this Life-Force Prana fills that void. They insist that it's not energy per se, although it may be the source of energy. They know it's there, yet we can't directly measure it. It is the energy source of the universe. It's the energy source that feeds our spiritual systems. It enables our prayers to be broadcast and heard. It's the food source of consciousness. It's the food source of our souls. It's what psychics use to conduct their magic. It's what shaman's use to heal. It's just there, and it has been ... forever.

Why this Prana is there, and how it is there, is unknown- - scientifically. We thus have no choice but to argue about it philosophically. Instantaneous healings, Jesus' miracles, children performing amazing stunts like having a thousand rosebuds open at once [Link 1206], etc., are the experimental evidence proving the existence of that Life-Force.

Physicists today have the same challenge explaining the system called our universe. Einstein's theory of relativity founded the big bang (which even he didn't buy into at the time). It also claims that the vacuum of space is not "nothing", but is instead a reservoir of a huge amount of energy. Each cubic centimeter (roughly the size of a thimble) of the vacuum of space contains 10^{96} units of energy. (That's 10 with 96 zeros after it.) That's an unbelievably huge number. This, too, was philosophically argued until Einstein's relativity was proven via experimental measurements.

In the mid 1960s the residual energy of the Big Bang was accidentally discovered by Bell Labs. The Holmdale Horn Antenna had been constructed to pick up intelligent-life signals from space.

Measuring the 7.23 Energy of the Big Bang

The Holmdale Horn Antenna

However, upon startup, they could not get rid of the background static. This is the same static that was always on our original TVs. It's called the Cosmic Microwave Background Radiation, and it has a wavelength of 7.23 cm [1].

This static is the smoking gun of the Big Bang. This accidental discovery immediately eliminated all the skeptics of the Big Bang and brought the scientific community together. The latest of these (Einstein's Theory of Relativity) proofs was announced in 2016, when the interaction of two black holes was measured.

These proofs, likewise, are evidence that the vacuum of space (the Prana) contains that enormous amount of energy. Lawrence Krauss [6] in his book "A Universe from Nothing" attempts to relate these concept to the everyday person - - that you indeed can get a lot of energy from "Nothing".

To explain how this is done, here is a quick math lesson for those who enjoy such:

Quick Math Lesson on Energy

$$1 = 1$$

Therefore: $$1 - 1 = 0$$

Written a Different Way:

$$(+1) + (-1) = 0 = \text{"Nothing"}$$

How "Nothing" Becomes Something

The above math is how science treats this hard-to-believe "Nothing". You can get a lot done using (+1), and you can get a lot done using (-1), i.e., these are simply different forms of energy. Yet, together they still add up to the "Nothing", i.e., they indeed add up to zero. Welcome to the back door of Einstein's relativity. The (+1) and the (-1) are (symbolically speaking) energy and dark energy, matter and anti-matter, etc. Per the actual relativity mathematics, the (+1) is the energies that we can see and feel (the light, motion, heat, etc.), whereas the (-1) is gravity. These are each powerful forms of energy, yet when combined (to become zero) they become the mystical Prana.

You and I, and everything around us, came from the Big Bang. Per Einstein's famous equation $E = mc^2$, our mass (m) is nothing more than energy (E). This means that we, too, came from that same mystical Prana.

In summary, we now have discussed the ancient Greeks' Ether, the spiritual world's Life-Force, and the modern-day physics' "Nothing". These are all different terms for the same thing - - and (once again) that is the mystical Prana.

We will continue this Prana discussion, but first let's discuss you and me more so.

1.2 We are Vibrational Beings

Back in Einstein's age, when Neils Bohr "invented" the Bohr atom (electrons orbiting around a nucleus), there were ongoing technical debates. On Mondays, Wednesdays, and Fridays, the electron was a particle. On Tuesdays, Thursdays, and Saturdays, it was a wave (just energy). A lot of famous scientific personalities, whose names are referenced daily in today's colleges, were essentially arguing whether we are really solid objects or if we are just energy. This was nearly one hundred years ago!

We are vibrational beings. A tiny fraction of the atom, and thus a tiny fraction of our bodies, is mass. The rest is vibrating energy. Per the discussion above, even that tiny bit of mass is ultimately energy.

The people on this planet are waking up more and more to this realization. For example, Dr. Masaru Emoto has completed studies on the formation of water crystals. Typical city tap-water does not yield any crystals upon slow freezing - - just a boring blob of ice. However, when the same water experiences music, it yields beautiful crystals. Such crystals also result when humans provide positive words and thoughts. This is clear evidence that we are vibrational beings (just like music), and our surroundings listen and respond to that energy.

When the Fukushima disaster recently occurred, people worldwide sent healing energy. They took on a spiritual approach by recognizing the power of their own vibrational energy. They also recognized the power of being united in consciousness. A similar outpouring of energy occurred on December 21, 2012, and likewise for the harmonic convergence of 1987. The list goes on and on.

Linda Madini sums this up for us [Link 1605]:

"It seems to me that this is a huge step forward in consciousness. More people than ever in history understand that we are vibrational beings.

What is a vibrational being?

Everything in the universe is in motion; nothing ever rests. Energy moves, vibrates and circles. Animate and inanimate objects have their own frequency of vibration. Human beings encompass body, mind and spirit. Each of these parts vibrates at a different level of frequency."

- - - - - - - -

1.3 The Prana of the Universe

The above quote is from a spiritual person very much into yoga, etc. She talks of the body, mind, and spirit being separate energies. Likewise, this my first mention of the word "consciousness". Is this, yet, another form of energy?

The following discussion sorts out these different energies, and in doing so, reveals the approach taken in this book.

The mystical Prana is always there. Thru things like Einstein's Big Bangs, it creates sine-wave energy.

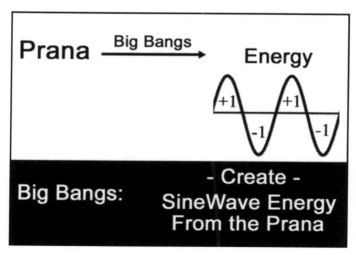

That sine wave has a (+1) and a (-1) aspect to it, and indeed adds up to zero - - as it should. That sine-wave energy is what created you and me and everything we know as our universe.

Of the Mind, Body, and Spirit, this is the Body. It is the energy that Bell Labs measured. It has a 7.23 cm wavelength. It is the smoking gun of the Big Bang.

Consciousness is very different. This is the middle portion of the following graph. Tools *within* you convert the Prana into consciousness. You can vary both the frequency and the intensity. (By contrast, Big Bangs produce a single fixed frequency.) You have choices. Of the Mind, Body, and Spirit, this is the Mind.

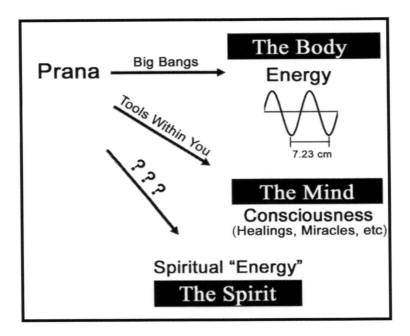

Finally, there's the Spirit aspect of the Prana. Perhaps the Prana is converted into Spiritual energy - - or the Prana itself is that Spiritual energy [Life-Force). Since we can't measure it, then any discussion is purely philosophical or religious.

1.4 The Approach Taken in this Book

Throughout this book I'll refer to the 7.23 cm energy quite often as the driving force of our universe. This implies that the Prana created the 7.23 and that, in turn, created our universe. Spiritual people will, and are certainly welcome to, take exception to this, arguing that consciousness created our universe instead. I agree, but for teaching a general audience, the first approach is much more teachable-friendly. That's because everyone understands energy, yet many people are uncomfortable talking about consciousness.

Regarding the Spirit energy, those are philosophical and religious discussions. Such is not part of this book. We define God as "that which we don't understand...yet".

Chapter 2
-The Flower of Life -

As described at the beginning of Chapter 1, the Flower of Life can be thought of as the mechanism inside the grandfather clock called our universe. It does not explain why we are here, but rather *how* we are here.

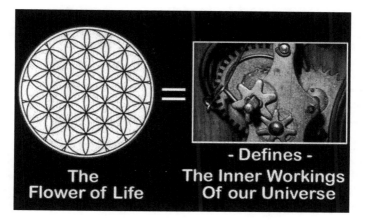

It's all about the math, and it's very simple math. The math of the Flower of Life is called Sacred Geometry. These lectures can be thought of as a review of ancient events, as well as current events, through that Sacred Geometry lens. This separates the real information from the non-real. It separates myths from truths.

Hermes is a mythical figure in ancient Greece. As you'll learn, he was also a real figure. Pythagoras (born 495 B.C.) is credited as being the founder of mathematics. It turns out that Hermes taught Pythagoras. He taught him Sacred Geometry, and this included a trip to the pyramids [1, 4].

Our body's structure is based on Sacred Geometry, e.g., the relative lengths of your arms and legs. This is why the Greek statues look so "true", unlike the subsequent Roman statues.

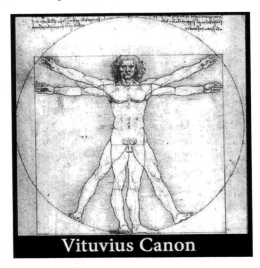

Vituvius Canon

Leonardo da Vinci's teacher was educated on this as well [1]. The famous picture above was drawn by da Vinci and depicts some Sacred Geometry aspects of our physical bodies.

2.1 The Tone-Plate Analogy

Now that you understand that the universe has its own source of energy (the "Nothing" or the Prana), and we are vibrational beings tapping that energy, I am now going to relate that to the Flower of Life and how it works.

My approach here is for you to imagine that the following tone-plate story is real. You are welcome to call it a myth. Nonetheless, this myth provides a much needed stepping-stone approach to help you understand the creation process, i.e., how that energy becomes you and me and the things around us. That's what the Flower of Life does.

Imagine you sprinkled sand onto a metal plate. Then, if you vibrate the plate with a single musical tone (note), such as the 7.23 cm, you get a pattern like the one shown below.

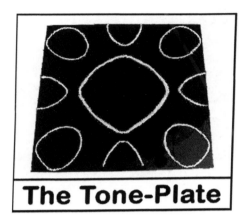

The Tone-Plate

Notice that the sand ends up only on the "lines", and there is no sand in the dark areas in between.

If you then blew all the sand away with a strong blast of air and sprinkled the plate again with more sand, the exact same pattern would reappear. Such tone-plate demonstrations are often done in physics classes today. Now let's allow this technology to help explain our universe

Notice how the four square edges seem to impact the resulting pattern, i.e., the "circles" aren't exactly circles.

Our universe is *infinite*. Therefore, it can't have "square edges". Thus the key question is what happens if you sprinkle sand onto a vibrating *infinite* plate?

Answer: You get the Flower of Life!

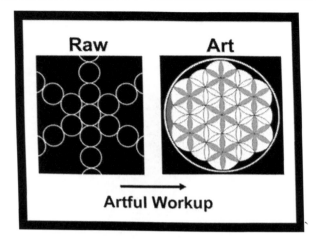

On the left is the raw tone-plate image for such an infinite plate. The drawing on the right is the artful workup (using a compass/pencil only) of that same pattern.

That same pattern is repeated over and over, yielding the bird's eye view of our infinite plate on the right (below).

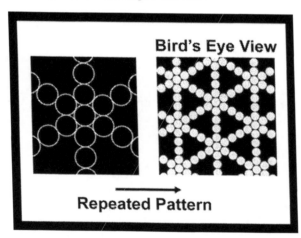

That infinite plate, with those zillions of repeating patterns, is our universe. If there is such a thing as another universe, then that universe has its own repeating pattern as well. That pattern is probably different from ours because their Flower of Life is probably different. By the end of this book, you'll also understand how those different Flowers of Life are possible. It's very simple. It has to be.

Therefore, as part of our mythological discussion here, imagine that our universe's energy has a constant tone (or note) equal to the 7.23 cm (the energy of the big bang discussed earlier). It is "on" all the time, and thus it creates this repetitive tone-plate pattern. That infinite array of repeated patterns is our universe.

How does this explain you and me?

Now imagine that each of these nodes is a seed, where a plant, a human, a planet, etc., grows! These are the things that you and I actually see in our daily lives. That's what the rest of this chapter is about. Even though each of these things grows very differently (from one another), that growth is *also* governed by the Flower of Life. These physical things may not "eat" the 7.23 cm energy at dinnertime. You eat food instead! However, that food ultimately came from the 7.23 cm energy of the Big Bang.

The scope of this chapter is not to give you a college course in physics. We simply want you to grasp the basic concepts of Sacred Geometry and that there is an energy source out there from which we are created and sustained.

With this in mind, we'll now give you the bottom line of how the Flower of Life is "everything", and why it's found in so many ancient structures.

2.2 Genesis (The Seed of Life)

The Bible is not exactly full of pictures, if you ever noticed. A few pictures would have gone a long way, at least for me. Here is the picture that should be in the very first book of the Bible.

Notice, in the above drawing, there are six circles surrounding the initial middle circle. These are the six "days" of creation in Genesis. At the end of the "sixth day" you have miraculously created this six-pedal flower, and then God rested.

Based on "Sacred Geometry", this can only be a six pedal, and not a five or seven pedal, flower. Here's why: When you draw Sacred Geometry by the human hand, the only tool you are allowed to use is a fixed-diameter compass. You have to start somewhere, so you simply draw the initial circle. That is simply a reference point "in the great void of nothingness". You then put the point of your compass on the only available reference point, and that's anywhere on the outer circumference of that original circle, and draw the second circle. Then, from this point forward, you simply put the tip of your compass at any and all intersection points (associated with the initial circle) and continue drawing new fixed-diameter circles. Via this method, you can only draw six outer circles, and that final circle completes the perfect six-pedal flower above.

2.3 The Egg of Life

The above two-dimensional Genesis pattern is often called the Seed of Life. We live in a three-dimensional world. Here is the same Genesis drawing, but in three-dimensions. (Put these on top of one another, and you'll see that the drawings are exactly the same.) You can readily see our original Genesis 6+1=7 spheres. What you cannot see is the eighth sphere (the seventh day) in the rear.

The Egg of Life

This is known as the Egg of Life, and for a very good reason. These original 8 cells are you. They are located at the base of your spine, in the exact middle of your body. Most people are aware that every cell in their body is replaced every seven years. That's true – except for these original 8 cells [1]. These remain in tack, unchanged, your entire life.

For learning purposes, imagine that the infinite plate pattern is always "on" as described earlier, but pretend that it is powered by electricity instead of the 7.23 cm energy. Thus it is an electrical grid. Now imagine that your original 8 cells are what (enable you to) "plug you into" that grid. From that pin-point forward, you grow (just like a plant grows from seed) into you. As you'll learn, your growth is *also* based on Sacred Geometry. You simply become another addition to our universe. The image on that TV screen now includes you.

Perhaps now, arguably, you have a revised grasp of what (the hard to grasp) Genesis is all about. If this 8-cell scenario is true for all animals, is it also true for all plants? Genesis implies that it's true for Mother Earth - - then why not everything in between? Does each rock, each grain of sand, etc., have such an egg or seed? Are these what "plug into" the 7.23 cm electrical outlet? Are you more comfortable calling it God's electrical outlet? Do these 8 original cells anchor your soul to your physical body? These are just questions to get you thinking.

2.4 *The Fruit of Life*

The Flower of Life hides a secret. Notice the "ring" truncates certain outer circles in the Figure below.

The "True" Flower of Life Has Additional Outer Rings

If you remove this "ring" (these rings have meaning that we will not discuss here), you expose the "entire" Flower of Life, and embedded in it is much more information.

Aristotle, another (hint) Greek philosopher born 384 B.C., taught the Flower of Life, yet was cautious about going "beyond" this outer ring. He discussed that only with his most trusted associates because of the sacred secrets it held [1].

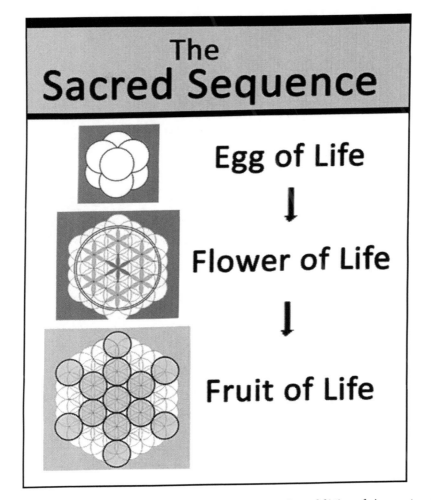

The
Sacred Sequence

Egg of Life

↓

Flower of Life

↓

Fruit of Life

What was "hidden" behind those rings were six additional important circles, in addition to the 7 shown on the Flower of Life. There are now 7+6 = 13 total important circles. The remaining (lighter) circles in the Fruit of Life above don't really exist. They were drawn in, using our compass, simply to help us place these critical 13 circles in their proper geometric positions.

In the next chapter, you'll (hopefully) become fascinated by the numbers 12 and 13. What's most important here, however, is what's revealed below.

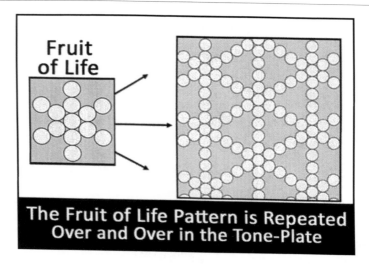

Fruit of Life

The Fruit of Life Pattern is Repeated Over and Over in the Tone-Plate

This 13 circle pattern is repeated over and over, to make the entire tone-plate pattern. Nothing else is needed. That is incredibly significant!

Thus the Fruit of Life (the arrangement of these 13 circles) is the true "building block" of our reality. Maybe you don't understand this, but you can at least understand the significance.

This is why Aristotle was so cautious about sharing it. Who knows, maybe he thought it might get in the hands of the wrong persons or space-invaders. Thus, the fact that I am sharing this with you here and now is likewise significant.

The Fruit of Life yields a vast amount of information. It should because everything is based on it. Whereas the Seed of Life (or Egg of Life) give you life itself (connects you to the God's electrical plug), the Fruit of Life is the inner workings of that TV. It literally determines your body's relative proportions, the shape of every crystal in the world, the shape of butterfly wings, how plants grow, and on and on. It determines all of the physical dimensioning of our reality.

2.5 Metatron's Cube

So far we have just drawn circles. Those are "female" (accept this as a definition for now). For the first time we are going to draw lines. We are going to put down our compass ("female" way) and use a straight edge ("male" way). We are not going to measure anything. We are just going to draw straight lines between the centers of the circles as shown below.

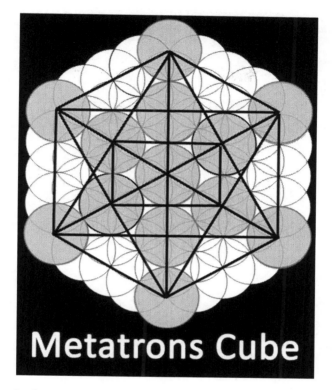

We have only drawn some of the lines. There are many more centers to be connected. Nonetheless, you can make out shapes, such as rectangles, triangles, the Star of David, etc. You can even visualize, or imagine, some three-dimensional objects. In reality, the Fruit of Life is a three dimensional object (like the Egg of Life) made up of spheres and not circles. Thus, there are many more spheres and many more lines.

These lines determine the structural dimensions of *everything* in our reality. They fix the relative lengths of everything, i.e., their ratios. This is remarkable if you let it sink in.

For example, there are 5 primary crystal-shapes that come out of the Fruit of Life, and indeed there are only these 5 primary crystals shapes discovered in our universe. These are shown below.

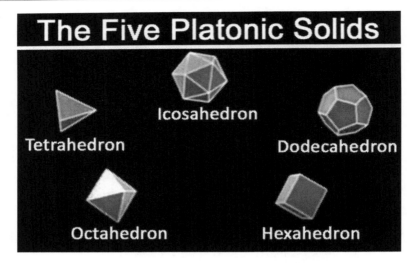

We not only find these in actual mineral crystals, but in things like snowflakes and energy field patterns. (By combining these, you come up with the 13 total Archimedean solids identified in our universe and studied in geometry.)

The above explains the structure of non-living things, but what about living things? The answer is the DNA molecule itself is a careful arrangement of stacked Sacred Geometry crystals. As the plant or animal grows, the DNA molecule itself provides detailed recipes for changing its form -- adding arms and legs, organs, leaves, flowers, pine cones, etc. These are the physical things that you and I see.

2.6 The Great Fall

The Great Fall in the Bible involves a crystal, a very big and very important crystal -- about the size of the Earth itself (We'll discuss it later). It was severely damaged thousands of years ago. A major piece of our history involves the steps taken to repair it and make it functional once again.

2.7 The Fibonacci Sequence

This is an extremely important section because it involves you. It involves action from you.

The "Fibonacci" is about how things grow. The answer is everything grows (whether it's "alive" or not) in accordance with the Fibonacci sequence.

The quickest way to teach you the Fibonacci concept is via the growth pattern of the Sneezewort plant shown here:

The Sneezewort Plant
Both Leaves & Branches
Follow the Fibonacci

As the sneezewort plant grows it has one branch, then there are 2, then 3, then 5, 8, etc. The exact same pattern is repeated in the number of leaves. That's the Fibonacci sequence.

It's is a numerical sequence of 1, 1, 3, 5, 8, 13, 21, 34, 55. The next number is always the sum of the last two. You never see 4 leaves or 6 or 14. It is always one of these Fibonacci numbers.

This is not just math for show. This is how *you* grow. The bones in your body grow accordingly. The following figure below shows your knuckles. Each has a Fibonacci length without exception.

2-3-5-8
The Fibonacci
At Work

Your hand, forearm, and upper arm continue this pattern. Seashells and pine cones are famous examples. The spiral pattern of galaxies, hurricanes, plants unfolding, and pinecones growing are additional examples. (The spiral patterns are the "female" version of the Fibonacci, i.e., curves instead of lines.)

Here is a table for you mathematicians, and you can see how the Fibonacci manifests itself.

Number of Leaves		Ratio
1		
1	1/1 =	1.00
2	2/1 =	2.00
3	3/2 =	1.50
5	2/3 =	1.67
8	8/5 =	1.600
13	13/8 =	1.625
21	21/13 =	1.6154
34	34/21 =	1.6190
55	55/34 =	1.6176
89	89/55 =	1.6182

The Fibonacci
Striving for
1.6182....

Simply divide any two sequential numbers - - and you (eventually) get the exact same answer - - about 1.6182. Then, in Chapter 16, you'll learn how this number is obtained from Sacred Geometry.

Regarding these lectures, the key point is: In order for "Jesus to come again", i.e., for us to blossom into "Heaven", a Fibonacci event needs to occur - - just like the Sneezewort plant finally flowering. We first need to become a very strongly unified "8", for example. Then we need to clearly understand and reconnect with our past, which is the "5". That's when we can finally graduate into the 13 flowers, i.e., our future.

Thus the Fibonacci is not something you simply study in the lab. It also impacts us, as a population, on both the global and universal levels. We'll devote a lot of time in these lectures to this topic, including Jesus and his association with this, after we cover our past history.

2.8 The Tree of Life

Our final topic here, regarding Sacred Geometry, is the Tree of Life. Most of you have at least heard these words spoken. It's Bible-talk and has something to do with people eating fruit.

What do seeds do? They grow into trees, which produce flowers, which yield fruit, which yield seeds once again.

We do the same cycle. The circular form below is the Seed of Life (The Genesis Pattern) as discussed earlier. Just like in the plant-world, it leads to the "Tree of Life", which yields the Flower of Life, which yields the Fruit of Life, which yields the Seed of Life once again.

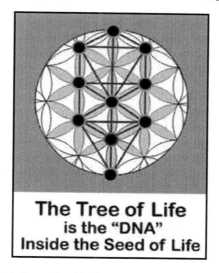

The Tree of Life
is the "DNA"
Inside the Seed of Life

Thus the Tree of Life is embedded in the Seed of Life, and that's what's reflected above.

If it helps, you can think of the "Tree of Life" as the "DNA" inside the seed.

In the Bible, Adam bit from the Tree of Life, as well as the Tree of Knowledge - - which is an interesting "twist" to the Tree of Life. The former caused us to pro-create (reproduce), and the latter caused problems. We cover both the Tree of Life and the Tree of Knowledge more so in Chapter 5 (Lucifer) and reference them throughout these lectures.

Summary

This completes our introduction to Sacred Geometry. We'll refer to these topics a lot in the following chapters.

Sacred Geometry is our human way of representing how the universe's energy manifests into actual physical items in our reality. The tone-plate is two dimensional, as are the drawings. Since our reality is three-dimensional, the real "tone-plate" is three dimensional. Thus, as difficult it is to perceive, our existence here is really just an image of that energy - - similar to a TV screen.

Back in Einstein's age, when Neils Bohr "invented" the Bohr atom (electrons orbiting around a nucleus), there were ongoing technical debates - - essentially arguing whether we are really solid objects or if we are just energy.

Thus the concept that we are just physical manifestations of energy is nothing new. In fact, Jesus' miracles were, arguably, his way of saying the same thing.

Chapter 3

- The Heavens -

In the very beginning of the last chapter, our energy discussion portrayed two different sources of energy in our universe. One is the mysterious prana energy (the life force) that is associated with the spiritual world. Yoga and meditation, for example, are heavily focused on breathing. Proper breathing techniques help assure that you are properly oriented to tap into this prana energy. You then convert it into another mysterious energy called consciousness. That energy, in turn, is the energy source for whatever will listen to it. Things do. Everything interacts. That cobweb of consciousness interactions is ruled by Sacred Geometry. It has an order, and that is our universe.

Philosophy and religions can take it from there. Since we can't actually measure (yet?) the prana life-force energy, this leaves it open to such debate.

This chapter is not about that mysterious prana energy. Instead this chapter is about the "Universe from Nothing" energy. We can measure this energy. The wavelength is 7.23 cm. This is the "cosmic microwave background radiation" which Bell Labs accidentally discovered in the late 1960s. It is the energy of the big bang and is the source of everything that we can observe and measure, in our everyday universe, from sub-atomic particles to black holes.

Now, let's talk about the Heavens. So far we've only talked about the energies associated with our world here on Earth.

Now, we need to talk about the Heavens......

3.1 The Piano

Bortolomeo Christofori (1655-1721) invented the piano. Here is a picture of the piano keys. Notice there are black keys and white keys. Also notice that there is repetition.

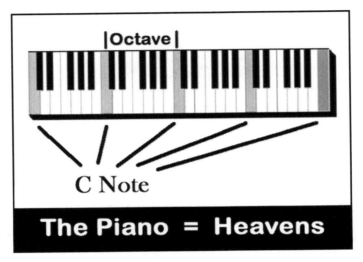

Each of these repetitions is called an octave, and we will talk about that aspect (of creation) later in this chapter. The far more important aspect is the twelve notes within a given octave. (Sometimes we'll say thirteen notes because it's convenient to include the first note of the next-higher octave).

Bortolomeo's depiction of the black and white keys is *exactly* how then heavens of our universe are structured. The white keys are the main keys. The black keys are used less, just as in the design of the piano.

No, this is not a crazy idea. In fact it is not an idea at all, but rather an exact mathematical (or musical) representation. Recall that we are vibrating beings. Strings vibrate as well. So it is no coincidence that music and the heavens have a relationship.

Whereas the Flower of Life (Sacred Geometry) determines what manifests itself (into the things we can touch and feel, for example) in our world of 7.23 cm, the "Piano of Life" (music) reveals the other worlds (such as where Angels come from) which exist around us, but at frequencies different from 7.23 cm. You can come back to this statement, but for now just keep reading and things will quickly become clearer.

You and I, and the world we are familiar with (i.e., 7.23 cm), is the equivalent of the E note on the piano. When hell, fire, damnation, and all that biblical fervor occurs and "Jesus comes again", we get to move up to the F note. This "move" is the underlying central topic in this book. Eventually we'll move up even higher notes into the Heavens. The Heavens, simply stated, are the higher notes.

It's really that simple. Thank God for Bortolomeo for, without the piano, this would be a much more difficult (technical) presentation.

When you strike a piano key, you get a specific musical note, vibration, frequency, wavelength, etc. These all mean the same. You don't need to be an expert in these to understand. These are also referred to as different levels or different dimensions when you get away from the piano and start talking about the heavens. Again, they all mean the same thing.

For the moment, we are going to use the term frequency because that is how you tune a radio - - by changing the frequency on your FM (frequency modulation) dial. The E frequency, which is where our world resides, is the 7.23 cm wavelength. That is our radio station, and what we perceive is that which is present on that frequency. The number itself is not important - - just the concept.

The angels in the Bible always come from the heavens. This means that the world they perceive is literally on a higher frequency FM station. The white notes above us are the heavens.

Exactly like tuning a radio, if you turned the dial and somehow tuned into one of these higher frequencies, you could literally see those Angels. Likewise, they can tune their radio dial to see you.

3.2 The Black Keys

Why are there black keys on the piano? The first note is a C, and the last (thirteenth) note is also a C note. Thus you have a low C note and a high C note. Mathematically, and this is the important part, the frequency of the High C is exactly double the frequency of the Low C. If, for example, the lower C has a frequency of 1, then the higher C has a frequency of 2. They are thus in perfect harmony with each other, and sound really good (essentially the same) when you strike them both at the same time.

Regarding the twelve notes in between, each one is roughly 1/12th of a step.

Again, why are some keys black and some white? The reason is simple. The white notes sound good when played together, and the black keys sound terrible when you mix them with the white keys, and especially the C note.

Thus, the white keys are in harmony with each other, but the black keys are non-harmonious. They interfere with the white keys. They interfere with the harmonious sound the white keys are attempting to make.

However, it is important to note that the black keys are still there. They are an inherent part of the piano, and they are an inherent part of our universe. For the moment simply think of them as "stepping-stones" to get across a creek, i.e., you spend very little time on them. The piano analogy is "jazz" players sometimes play these black keys. However, they spend very little time on them before coming back to the white keys.

3.3 The Law of Twelve

Notice that we have twelve months, twelve gates, twelve tribes, twelve apostles, twelve signs of the zodiac. There were even twelve Knights of the Round Table. There also are twelve planets if you include the sun and our moon as such, which is the case in ancient hieroglyphic types of text. Sure, you can disagree with any of these "twelves", but as a whole, they sure make you raise your eyebrows.

There are also twelve chakras in your body. Chakras are the spiritual nodes (spiritual centers) in your body. These tap into the mysterious prana energy. This is what meditating and magical healings are all about.

3.4 Chakras vs. The Piano

We'll cover chakras later when we discuss Jesus' miracles. Here we'll reveal the astonishing similarity to the piano.

Technically the "chromatic" scale in music is all twelve notes (the thirteenth note, i.e., the high C, is the beginning of the next octave.) Your body has twelve chakras. The low C (chakra) is at the base of your body (near the original 8 cells), and the high C is at the top of your body just above your head. However, of these twelve there are seven primary chakras, and they correspond exactly to the white keys on the piano. This is called the "major scale" on the piano.

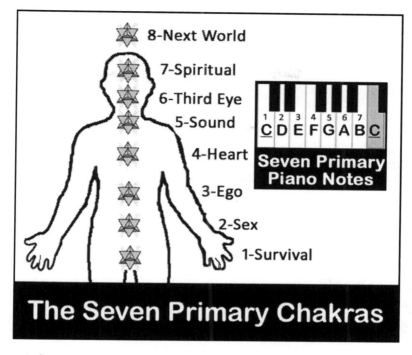

The Seven Primary Chakras

As an infant you get more and more "in-tune" with each chakra as you grow up - - starting at the bottom. As an adult you (via meditations, etc.) try to get more and more in tune with the higher chakras.

Most teachers and students of the chakra system focus on these seven primary chakras, i.e., the "major scale". The remaining five chakras are the equivalent of the black notes on the piano. These are for advanced meditators, and just like the black notes on the piano - - they are like stepping stones, i.e., you don't spend any time there because they are disharmonious. It's quick in, quick out.

Furthermore, the 13th note on the piano is the beginning of the next octave. We actually have thirteen chakras; however, that 13th one is not accessible because it is literally the beginning of the next universe. Believe it or not, just like there are multiple octaves on the piano, there are multiple universes. Science is beginning to recognize this as well. Lawrence Krauss in *A Universe from Nothing* mentions such.

The parallels between the chakras, the piano, all the twelves, and our universe are collectively quite astonishing. My point is this is no coincidence, and it's time for us to wake up and realize that our future critically depends on us waking up and getting aligned. A later chapter is indeed titled *Getting Aligned.*

Now we are going to move on. We have established the "Heavens". Now let's discuss the residents of those Heavens.

3.5 Giants & the Fibonacci

There were giants in the Bible, and they came from the heavens. The terms giants and heavens seem to be linked. What's *that* all about?

The answer is simple. The higher the frequency, the larger the beast. When mankind finally moves from the E note to the F-note, we'll be about 10-15 feet tall. When we thereafter go to the G note, we'll be about 35 feet tall. After that it's about 55 feet tall. These types of giants are talked about in the Old Testament. Other ancient texts, such as the Sumerian texts and the Dead Sea Scrolls, have the same stories. In Egypt, there are statues for each of these heights. Egypt was a school for teaching the different levels (frequencies) of the heavens, and they knew much more about it then than we do now.

Now we are going to present a mathematical link that helps explain what's going on, i.e., why do the Angels get so much bigger as you move up into the Heavens?

We know that Sacred Geometry plays a major role in the physical structure and growth of humans, plants, animals, etc. Thus it seems reasonable (a hypothesis) that the same must be true for the heavens.

The key question now becomes: what is the mathematical relationship between the size of these giants and their level-in-the-heavens. The Egyptian statues are a good source of data because they represent humans (who now reside at) the higher levels. This is well documented [1]. They are also staring you in the face when you visit Egypt, so you can actually measure their size.

I thus compared the height of the Egyptian statues to the properties of the piano. I tested (trial and error) many different relationships between these two. Thus the frequency, wavelength, binary sequence, Fibonacci sequence, and all the possible combinations of these, were investigated for both the chromatic scale and the major scale. Remarkably, the only relationship that predicted these statue heights with any kind of accuracy was the Fibonacci sequence, and it did so very well. Every other sequence or combination failed miserably to give any correlation.

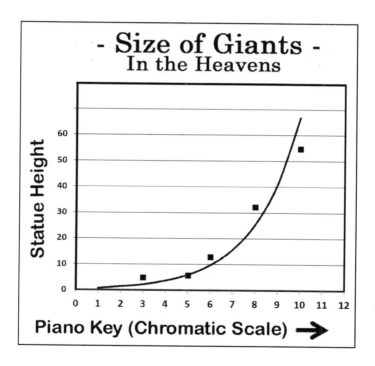

Figure 3-4. "Moving Up into the Heavens" is a Fibonacci-Based Event. The Solid line (predicted Giant Heights) closely matches the known sizes of the Giants (squares)

For those of you who enjoy graphs, the solid line in the above graph is the predicted Fibonacci height of the giants, and the little squares are the actual heights of the giants (Egyptian statues). By scientific standards, the agreement is very good, if not excellent.

This is powerful evidence that moving up into the Heavens is indeed a Fibonacci event - - as it should be. It should be based on Sacred Geometry, and that's what this graph says.

For those of you not comfortable with graphs, what is stated here is that the height of Angels in the heavens increases in the same way that your knuckle-lengths increase.

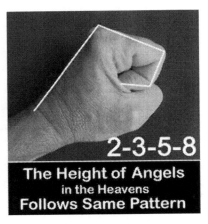

Figure 3-5. Your Knuckle-Lengths follow a Fibonacci Pattern- - and so do the Height of Angels as you go up into the Heavens.

3.6 Moving Up in the Heavens

There's little doubt in my mind that Jesus fully understood the heavens, and thus timed his arrival and teachings accordingly - - to help us through the upcoming transition. (We cover Jesus' timing in Chapter 9). This is the rapture event talked about in the Bible. It's 2012. It's when Jesus "comes again". However, if you get away from all the religious fervor, the transition to the next level is a mathematical event. Per the Fibonacci math, we have to add two numbers together and the result is the new us.

What does this mean? To help answer this, let's revisit the sneezewort plant from Chapter 2.

The sneezewort plant remembered that it had 5 leaves and then it had 8. It used these two numbers to then create the 13 new leaves.

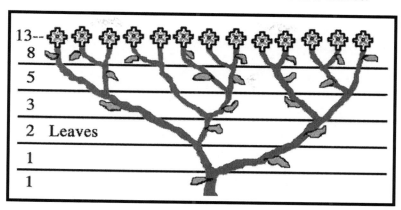

We have to do the same. We have to "remember". As stated in the prior chapter, we not only have to become a good unified "8", we also have to remember our past "5" - - and to participate in, and encourage, the concerted effort to combine these two. This message is also emphasized by Drunvalo [Link 102]

This implies that we are not going to have a successful 2012 event (or rapture or Jesus "coming again") unless we clearly understand this Fibonacci event, and successfully make it happen.

To do that, we first need to understand our past.

The next several chapters are that past. Let's begin.

Chapter 4

-The Consciousness Grid -

In the 1960s Ivan T. Sanderson [Link 401] took push-pins and placed them on the globe where airplanes and ships had disappeared without a trace. He went back to the very first days of aviation and well before that for the maritime disappearances.

His work appeared in the April 1971 issue of SITU's journal, Pursuit. Sanderson then published the article "The Twelve Devil's Graveyards around the World" for a 1972 issue of Saga magazine.

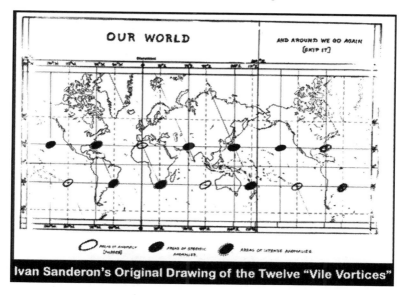

Ivan Sanderon's Original Drawing of the Twelve "Vile Vortices"

His original diagram (above) shows the Bermuda Triangle as one cluster-point. The Devil's Triangle near Japan is another. However, to his surprise, the push-pins statistically clustered around ten locations. Then he was amazed to discover that these ten locations were equal distance from each other and equal distance from the equator. Two other locations were the North and South Poles. Combined, bringing the total to twelve, these form an icosahedron. Unknown to him at the time, an icosahedron is one of the Sacred Geometry crystal shapes.

Prior to that in the 1920s, Alfred Watkins became famous for studying the alignment of sacred structures and sites in England and nearby. He carefully measured the location layout of ancient structures such as monuments, megaliths, ridgetops and waterfords. He found they were constructed along straight lines over very long distances.

Others followed suite and measured more ley lines around the world, and also the location of 4,000 known sacred sites (pyramids, temples, mounds, etc.). These form a more detailed crystal shape as depicted below.

Ivan Sanderson's original icosahedron is obtained by connecting the white dots. The 5-sided "caps" around each of these dots collectively form a stellated dodecahedron-icosahedron.

This is often called the Christ Consciousness Grid because the 5th note on the piano (the G note) is the Christ Consciousness note, i.e., "Heaven". This is ultimately where we are headed in this transition. More on these topics later.

_____

Finally, about 1980 Carl Munck investigated the GPS coordinates of these ancient structures. Using the Great Pyramid as his zero-reference point, he calculated his own set of GPS coordinates from there.

He then compared those coordinates to the actual structures. He suspected there might be a code to the structure's actual length and width, number of steps, number of sides, etc. Using only these numbers, he simply multiplied (or divided) them together, and what he got was astonishing. There, on the outside of every structure, was that code - - via simple multiplication -- giving the exact longitude and latitude of their own unique GPS position.

That code only works if the Great Pyramid is your zero-reference point. This tells you a lot about the Great Pyramid. Indeed, it serves several important functions in our world.

_____

This is our past. Thus the ancient cultures knew much more about our past, and what it's all about, than we do. Indigenous cultures today still know much more about our past than we do.

Although the modern world has just "discovered" our own earthly grid, spirit science knows that such grids are everywhere in the universe, including other dimensions.

4.1 What Consciousness Grids Do

A species cannot exist without its own consciousness grid [1]. In this sense, grids define what is a species. The universe is like a huge circuit board with all these interacting grids, chakras, etc. Grids are thus a big part of this overall network called our universe. That entire circuit board or network is based on Sacred Geometry.

Note that this Consciousness Grid is specific to the human species, yet it's around the earth. This tells you that we have a unique relationship with Mother Earth. This relationship has been long forgotten by most of us, yet it is an extremely important part of this upcoming 2012 transition. Thus it is important for you to understand that relationship, and this book provides such.

The Consciousness Grid is *also* an extremely important part of this transition, and indeed it's mentioned throughout the rest of this book.

Here we provide a few more examples of the Grid's characteristics.

Ken Keyes, Jr., wrote the book The Hundredth Monkey. It describes research where monkeys were being raised on Japanese Islands. They were often fed sweet potatoes. An eighteen month-old baby monkey learned how to wash her potatoes in water - - to get rid of the undesirable sand. Other children quickly learned from her, and those children taught their parents.

Then (and this is the key point) at the start of the seventh year, several other islands simultaneously - - and quickly - - learned to wash theirs. This was a first, baffling the scientists who suggested that there must be some kind of genetics-related force field that stretched across these distant islands.

A very controlled experiment was later performed using humans: A group of people looked at pictures in Australia while those same pictures were broadcasted in Britain [1] - - thousands of miles away. A given picture contained many faces, most of which were hard to pick out. However, only minutes after the broadcast in Britain, the Australians could readily pick out most of the faces. The conclusion was that humans are connected somehow and in real time.

———

Another phenomenon is the Bermuda Triangle. It is one of the twelve nodes of the Consciousness Grid. Planes have disappeared. That's exactly what happened. They went through a portal, a place where you can go to another dimension or another time.

Einstein's relativity fully supports such strange phenomena as portals and time travel.

We (humans) have been doing time travel since the mid 1940s. See the movie *The Philadelphia Experiment* and check out *Al Biedek* on the web. This was during World War II on Oct 28, 1943. The goal was to make a ship disappear from the enemy - - literally. Horrifically, there were a few sailors stationed on that ship, the *USS Eldridge*, during the actual test. *Al Beidek* (was one of two who) jumped off the ship to escape the electrical inferno. Moments later he was in 1985 and in Norfolk, Virginia - - 200 miles away. He was able to return because the same scientist was there (with a much better machine) to send him back in time (that scientist had aged the 40 years). Thus Al Beidek, and his mate who had also jumped ship, were the first humans to teleport.

Thus not only have humans teleported, that's possibly what has happened to (at least) a few of the many planes, boats, etc., that have disappeared at the nodes on the Consciousness Grid.

4.2 The Bible & the Grid

Even though the Grid is not referenced in the Bible, both the Great Fall and "Heaven" are directly related to it. The Grid is a huge part of our past. It has a major influence on the present, and especially on the "day of reckoning". The indigenous tribes know it well.

We'll cover that history in Chapters 6 and 7.

Chapter 5

- Lucifer -

This chapter is on Lucifer. This is very much a part of our history, yet it's also a very relevant Sacred Geometry item.

5.1 Sacred Geometry Aspect

Recall our Flower of Life discussion in Chapter 2. Our universe has a known frequency of 7.23 cm, and when that "note" is played, we get the Flower of Life.

It turns out that there are actually *two* solutions to Flower of Life "math". Here they are side by side.

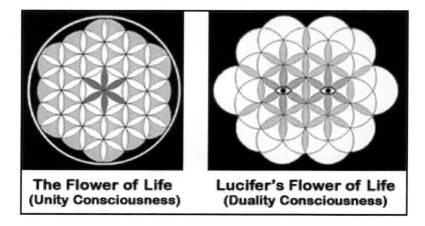

The Flower of Life
(Unity Consciousness)

Lucifer's Flower of Life
(Duality Consciousness)

Figure 5-1. Lucifer's Flower of Life has Dual "Centers", which leads to Duality Consciousness.

The one on the left is the unity consciousness, and reflects oneness with God, i.e., there is a single center. The one on the right has two "centers". It's duality consciousness. Guess which one we are? We are not of unity consciousness. That is what Jesus wants us to become. We, instead, are the Flower of Life on the right!

Our consciousness is thus split. Instead of operating purely from our heart (the "female" way) and simply doing what is right (unity consciousness), we can also operate from our mind (the "male" way), and that means we have choices.

In other words we have free will.

Let's first briefly visit the "math" of this free will. As stated previously, you draw Sacred Geometry (the Flower of Life) with a fixed-diameter compass. The only other rule is you have to put the "needle" end of the compass on (already existing) intersections of your lines. That's it! You can draw both of the above patterns with these simple rules. Please note that God did not use a compass to create the Flower of Life! It just so happens that you can replicate what he did using such simple rules. Thus the tone-plate, and under the right circumstances, will indeed yield the image on the right.

5.2 Lucifer Himself

Per Drunvalo [1] "God created Lucifer so that free will would exist". Lucifer did it his way by creating the Flower of Life on the right. Thus mathematically, Lucifer found another solution to the "equations" of the universe.

Per the Bible, God didn't seem too happy with Lucifer's approach. I certainly don't have the authority to take any side in this argument. I'll simply emphasize that we indeed have free will as a result of this experiment, which means that any of the bad things we do are done via our own choices.

Likewise, it is very difficult for any of us to go through life without judging others. Judging is a direct result of this duality (polarity) consciousness. When you judge, you are deciding what's right or wrong, good or bad, good or evil.

Unity consciousness requires us to see only the good in others, i.e., treat them as if they were part of you. We have to practice unity consciousness because we are naturally in polarity consciousness. It takes work. It takes commitment. Respect the views of others. Learn from them, and in doing so, they may also learn from you. The wholeness improves, rather than just the individual. There are no "experts" in the universe, except perhaps God himself. Even Lucifer blew it (depending on your views), and he was one of God's best, if not *the best,* Angel. But they will learn from this free will experiment, and the wholeness of the universe will, no doubt, benefit. Was that their plan all along?

5.3 Tree of Life vs. Tree of Knowledge

Recall that the Tree of Life was embedded in the Seed of Life, and I suggested (if it helps) to think of the Tree of Life as the DNA inside the seed.

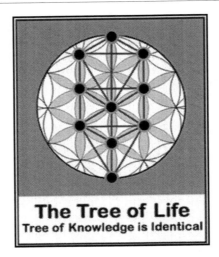

The Tree of Life
Tree of Knowledge is Identical

The Tree of Knowledge is that same "Tree" but it's the comparable one from Lucifer's Flower of Life. It is based on free will instead of pure unity consciousness.

When the Adam and Eve story occurs, they "bit" from the Tree of Knowledge. This means they crossed over, somehow, into duality consciousness from unity consciousness. You can use your imagination to figure out how such might occur. I am not going to get involved in this debate, so I'll be a comedian and say that ET (from the movie) was of unity consciousness. He mated with a very intelligent female ape, just after finishing a nice meal of (unusually large) BBQ'd ribs. His kids were unusually large and had anger issues right off the bat, something he'd never witnessed before.

The anger management issues result from the duality consciousness, which also creates the ego. The ego is famous for caring for itself, its family, and maybe a few close friends. Everyone and everything else, however, is fair game. This is the consequence of free will, the consequence of duality consciousness, and the consequence of Lucifer's experiment.

5.4 Does Lucifer explain Satan?

The Lucifer Experiment does explain our ego, and how we can get mixed up with the wrong group of people, etc., and then act like a bunch of testosterone-driven idiots. For me, these idiots are simply victims of this experiment conducted by Lucifer, yet endorsed by God.

In my opinion, the most suitable "Satan" explanation is the darkness/light aspect of our fundamental existence. Anytime anyone does an affirmation, meditation, etc., they (through their intentions) surround themselves with bright white light to keep the darkness and its associated consequences away. This is extremely important. Even Thoth in *The Emerald Tablets* [4] (we'll cover this in Chapter 13) provides ancient instruction to this same effect, in order to determine if what is bothering you (or possessing you) is this darkness or something else. When Native Americans do a "Vision Quest", they often put a circle of stones around themselves to achieve the same end. I had my own experience, when I forgot to do such, and had a memorable frightening experience. This "definition" is consistent with that of Pope John Paul II, as well as Billy Graham [Link 501]. They both say that hell is living in the absence of God, i.e., the absence of light, and is purely the consequence of your choice. Like counting to three, it is incredibly easy to surround yourself with the white light.

You just have to do it.

Thus take your ship out of the harbor and sail around. Just remember to bring this light with you, and you'll be just fine!

We cover the more technical aspect of darkness/light in Chapter 9.

Also remember that 2012 is about many things, and at the heart of it all is us moving into unity consciousness. When that happens, all of these Lucifer and Satan issues will simply dissolve and disappear. That's the math at work. So we are past the point now of debating such philosophical or religious difference, and we need to instead focus on increasing our unity consciousness

Thank You !

Tom Price

- Getting Aligned -
For the Planetary Transformation

Part II: History

- CHAPTERS -

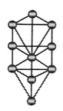

Chapter 6

- History of the Earth -

The Bible talks about fallen Angels, Adam and Eve, and the Great Flood in a few sentences. Apart from these and a couple of phrases about chariots from the sky, there is not much to go on regarding the ancient history of the Earth. Furthermore, these topics are talked about symbolically.

In this chapter, I will provide some incredibly relevant history that you will likely find difficult to swallow. Now, unfortunately, I have no choice (since no math is involved) but to throw some pretty crazy stuff at you, and hope that you don't slam the door. You are going to think I'm nuts. You are going to deny and resist.

Nonetheless, for the sake of mankind's progress, these things need to be said. Thus, so you don't feel backed into a corner, I'm providing choices.

So here we go. Here are two brief histories of ancient mankind from very different sources.

6.1 The History of the Earth

The cosmos is full of life including beings like us. There are about *two hundred and fifty thousand* such cultures anxiously watching the events unfold here on Earth [Link 1501] as I write this. That's because the events that have happened here on Earth are so unique in the universe (the Great Fall and more). Earth is literally on center stage. There are only a handful of these cultures that we've actually seen, and that's because they are on the same "piano note" we are. The rest reside at the higher frequencies, so they are invisible to us. With the exception of a couple, these are all good cultures as they reside in unity consciousness. Some cultures have done unbelievable things to help you and me.

However, the main point of this chapter is to discuss the bad-guys. One of these cultures is likely the result of another Lucifer-type experiment that has gone terribly wrong [Link 101]. They are not of unity consciousness. They are not of duality consciousness. They are pure ego, i.e., "unity" consciousness but of the wrong kind - - of the mind and not the heart. Like us swatting bugs, it does not faze them at all to kill us, and they have. If there is a "Satan", it's these guys (and girls) - - hook, line, and sinker. They are like robots. They are just doing what they do without remorse. They are nothing but ego. They are control freaks. They want to control us. They want to control the world.

They have no timeframe. They just keep at it. They are here now. They are among us. They, or at least their actions or the result of their actions, are on TV every day.

Per Drunvalo [1], there is nothing to worry about. In fact worrying is the wrong approach. Fear is the primary tool they use to control us. All this badness is *supposed* to be happening. It's normal. The goodness is increasing as well, and will win out. More on this topic later.

I present below two separate versions of the Earth's ancient history. These are from the bad-guys' perspective and the good-guys' perspective, respectively. Thus one is from the light side's perspective and the other is from the dark side's perspective.

My hope is you'll get interested enough to do some research on your own.

--The Past History of Earth (Version B)

During the time of the early solar system, there was an event in a far away star system called Lyra. The bad-guys destroyed one or more planets, and those refugees had to go somewhere. Some of the Lyrians wound up on Mars. Thereafter the bad-guys showed up in our early solar system, and they nudged a planet-sized comet (which is made up of ice) so that it would destroy the inhabited Mars. It missed Mars, but stripped it of its atmosphere. A planet in between Mars and Earth, called Maldek, was destroyed. It simply exploded, due to the near-miss, and became the asteroid belt. Earth was spared, but underwent major changes. Unlike Mars, this event actually helped create our atmosphere and land masses. Finally, the comet itself became Venus.

Suddenly Earth looked more desirable, and the bad-guys (at least some of them) made it their home. They settled in Lemuria which is the land mass containing the Southern Pacific Islands, including Australia. It was much larger then - - a large continent.

Meanwhile other Lyrian refugees (not the ones on Mars) hopped around and eventually made it to Earth as well, and set up what we know as Atlantis. So now we have the good-guys in the Atlantic and the bad-guys in the Pacific, and the Martians onlookers still camping out on Mars.

Hooray for the Atlanteans because they destroyed (sank) Lemuria. I'm assuming they used a comet or meteor, as that seemed to be the weapon of choice in those days. The remaining bad-guys actually went underground. (Lots of cultures choose to live underground because it is much safer.) The Martians (the other Lyrian refugees) finally came to Earth and settled in Sumer.

Regarding the Adam and Eve story, the bad-guys, who were grossly outnumbered, turned to human hybridization as their tool for controlling the Earth. Sumer became the location of that hybridization, and Homo sapiens were borne.

What's above (History of the Earth: Version B) is the bad-guy version of our history. It's from a person who had worked for the bad-guys - - and then left them.

These beings are here. They interfere with our lives daily. They are among us. They are on TV. They interbreed with us. These are the wealthiest people on Earth, and by far.

--History of the Earth (Version A)

We are virtually 100% certain that we've made it, i.e., the good-guys will win. The question is who are we, and what's *our* version of the Earth's History. In this case the "we" is not only you and me, but also those who are helping us and overseeing us. They are not on TV or in the news, and they do not interfere with our day to day events. That's because the good-rules are: you can lead a horse to water but you cannot make it drink. In other words, they are not supposed to interfere with our free-will. They need special permission to do so. Only the bad-guys blatantly interfere - - and without permission. In many ways, that's the definition of "bad".

With this in mind, here is the "good-guys" history. It is nicely summarized by Drunvalo [1], and it involves the Nephilim. Both the Bible and the Sumerian Tablets talk about the Nephilim. (This is no surprise as the Sumerian Tablets predate the Bible by about 3000 years.).

The Nephilim came from Nibiru, which is a planet that's part of our solar system. You don't know much about it because it's a rogue planet. It spends time near us, and then zooms back out into far space. Then it returns in another 3600 years or so. It never comes back to the same spot, which is bad news because on the next return, it might just crash into one of our nearby planets - - or even us. In the past, per the Sumerian Tablets, one of its moons *indeed* crashed into the planet Maldek, creating the asteroid belt.

Per the Sumerian Tablets, the Nephilim were about 10-12 feet tall. They needed gold to repair their planet's climate issue. Gold molecules in the atmosphere serve to reflect the heat back onto their planet, keeping the planet warm. This seems sensible as their planet would go far into space, away from our sun's heat.

They came to Earth to harvest that gold as told by Michael Tellinger in his book *African Temples of the Anunnaki: The Lost Technologies of the Gold Mines of Enki*. The geological evidence is indisputably there in Southern Africa [Link 601, Link 101]. There are precision-drilled horizontal mine shafts, discovered by modern mining operations, miles underground. On the surface are hundreds of rock formations creating measurable energy waves, not unlike pyramids do today. The hypothesis is this energy was used to somehow transport the gold onto the spaceships.

After mining it themselves for hundreds of thousands of years, they decided (about 200,000 years ago) to make slaves of the rather-backwards human species that were here, so they genetically modified them and created a new species - - and the homo-sapiens were born. This was no simple task. They needed permission and they got it. The Flower of Life was directly incorporated in the ceremony/conception process. It took, per Drunvalo [1], about 2000 years before the first batch "hatched". This new species was intentionally sterile. Apparently we make great slaves, as they used us for roughly 150,000 years! The slaves were intentionally kept on an island off the west coast of Africa.

The Adam and Eve story is about how Adam and Eve "cheated" and thus began reproducing. You can fill in the blanks here as you choose, or read Drunvalo's material or the Sumerian Tablets.

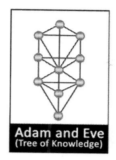

Figure 6-1. Adam and Eve Bit of the Tree of Knowledge

Regardless, they had bitten of the Tree of Knowledge, meaning they were now of duality consciousness, and with this are naturally part of the Tree of Life. The latter simply means that they can "go to our Heaven", as opposed to (my wild guess) going to doggy heaven.

Thus there were two strains: the (sterile) slave population and the Adam and Eve (pro-creating) population.

Eventually, due to natural events shifting the land masses on the Earth, that African island sank and at the same time Lemuria popped up in the Pacific. The descendents of Adam and Eve were relocated there, onto Lemuria, and left to grow on their own. Interestingly, some rather exceptional spiritual leaders came to be, and started teaching and assisting them on Lemuria.

Eventually, due to more Earth land masses shifting (obviously a regular event on Earth), Lemuria then sank, and Atlantis rose up at the same time. The leaders took advantage of this opportunity and physically created the Tree of Life on Atlantis by locating ten cities, and the like, at the appropriate locations. That's the Atlantis that we read about.

6.2 Comparing These Histories

As far as planets and comets hitting one another, and whether or not there is a Nibiru, all that will be worked out by science. All indigenous tribes talk about Atlantis [1], and how they got into boats and moved elsewhere following a great flood. Plato brought Atlantis to the attention of the modern world in 330 B.C. via his fictional stories.

The Nephilim used traditional spaceships and the Bible has references to such. I was shocked when I saw ancient drawings of spaceships with flames coming out the back! That means they used fossil fuels -- just like us. Thus they were not super advanced. However, they were more advanced than we are today, for sure.

The geological record has homo-sapiens "coming out of nowhere" about 200,000 years ago. This, too, matches the Nephilim stories.

However, we also know that the "bad-guys" are here and are among us. There are many layers to this "onion", and the most obvious is the Elite, i.e., the 1% that owns nearly all of the wealth on this planet.

The two histories differ primarily on the details of the bad-guys. However, Drunvalo clarifies that for us. The bad-guys indeed blew up planets elsewhere in our galaxy, and then came here. They did not go to Lemuria and then underground. They instead went to Mars, and ruined its atmosphere. (There is plenty of evidence of wars on Mars. See John E. Brandenburg's *Death on Mars: The Discovery of a Planetary Nuclear* Massacre.) After that they simply waited -- perhaps thousands or tens of thousands of years -- until the right opportunity arose. Then they "attacked" Atlantis, and became part of our DNA. Chapter 14 discusses this "attack". For the moment it means they became an inherent part of the human race, rather than an enemy that we can point to and shoot.

6.3 The Bad Guys

Recall that Lucifer was allowed to run his experiment here in our reality, and thus created polarity consciousness. Atlantis was also operating under Lucifer's experiment and seemed to be doing just fine (at least until the end per Plato). Likewise, you and I are operating under Lucifer's experiment, and (if you separate out the bad-guy behavior that's among us) we are generally doing OK. We just have to often remind ourselves that we need to think with our hearts, and not so much with our minds. We have to remind ourselves that we need to replace duality (polarity) consciousness with unity consciousness.

Per Drunvalo, experiments in free will have been allowed two or three times in the past, and they have always proven disastrous. It's bad enough here on Earth that we have husbands beating their wives and kids. However, this is absolute peanuts compared to the behavior of these bad-guys. They are pure male energies (no emotions) and, like Terminator in the movie, will stop at nothing. Look around and you'll see that they are being very successful. They don't have a timeline. They just keep at it, slowly but surely.

Jesus died on the cross, and planned to do exactly that (and more that we discuss in Chapter 13) to get our undivided attention - - to drive home the directive that we need to replace polarity consciousness with unity consciousness. His preachings were exactly this.

Every religion in the world knows we need to replace polarity consciousness with unity consciousness. That's the bottom line. It's awareness and then taking some kind of daily action to knowingly acknowledge and support that end.

The world of the bad-guys will simultaneously crumble away if we do this. This crumbling is purely a fringe benefit. (We'll cover this in Chapter 9). Trust me, they know this as well, and have tried everything possible to prevent it. You'd be shocked. They are incredibly smart, beyond your wildest imagination. Controlling religion has been a major part of their multi-faceted agenda.

Something else has become very clear to me: The universe is not "perfect". In many ways it's just like running a business. You have experiments being run, such as Lucifer's. There is also a "quality control" department. When there are problems people come to the rescue. Jesus is a great example. In Atlantis, or even before, those hybrids (Adam and Eve's offspring) actually got teachers who worked with them on learning how to ascend, and taking action to actually make it happen. Where did *they* come from (the teachers)? This is in the pre-Jesus days. Those teachers, just like Jesus, came from higher levels on the "piano".

Perhaps these QC issues are just 0.01%, and the other 99.99% of the universe is indeed "perfect". Who knows? I certainly don't. Nonetheless I feel very blessed that Jesus and this QC department are on our side and are working diligently to see us through this major mess.

The next chapter provides clarity on what caused this mess.

Chapter 7

- The Great Fall -

Everything was going just fine in Atlantis. They were in good hands and were collectively working on their spiritual science. The entire continent of Atlantis was working on it. As previously stated, all the cities were arranged in a Tree of Life pattern, and virtually every person participated. They were making good progress to shift from duality consciousness to unity consciousness.

Then, just before about 26,000 years ago, the bad-guys intervened on Earth for the first time. After they messed up Mars, and destroyed its atmosphere, they seized the opportunity and not only showed up at Atlantis, but showed up at a very vulnerable moment [Link 101].

These guys are very intelligent and very patient. Because of their low numbers, they choose situations where they can greatly leverage their power. In this case, and just like Adam and Eve, they "bit of the Tree of Life" of the Atlanteans. They thus became a permanent part of the Atlanteans, and thus you and me. Chapter 14 discusses this more so.

However, the real damage came when they built a machine, a pyramid that could help them get complete control of the planet, on the western end of Atlantis. Pyramids are built according to Sacred Geometry to tap the 7.23 cm wavelength energy of the universe. Think of pyramids as power generators. They "plug into" the universe and then use that power to do this or that. In this case the bad-guys were doing their own "Lucifer experiment", and creating a reality that would provide them total control of the planet and its residents.

Think about this for a moment and let it sink in. It was a "*man-made*" machine that was going to create a synthetic Lucifer-type reality. It better work correctly or you might have a disaster of unbelievable proportions on your hands. That's exactly what happened. They turned it on, lost control of it, and created a disaster beyond anything you could imagine. The remnants today are the Bermuda Triangle [Link 101], and that man-made pyramid is located underwater near Bimini. This was about 13,000 years ago.

Per Drunvalo [1] "It ripped open the lower dimensional levels of the Earth - - not the higher ones, but the lower ones". From a Sacred Geometry perspective, holes were ripped open between the 3rd and 4th level consciousness grids. Spirits, that did not normally have bodies, suddenly sought bodies to reside in. Thus they entered the bodies of the Atlanteans. Everyone was possessed, not with "the devil", or any such nonsense, but rather with entities from Earth who were scared, frightened, and lost. Everyone was affected. It was catastrophic.

The Atlanteans, prior to this disaster, were "young" 3rd dimensional beings. They had excitedly rounded first base and were well on their way to second base - - on their way to becoming 4th dimensional beings.

This disaster destroyed the ballpark, so to speak, and they had to start over. They were back at square one. That's us! It normally takes about 100,000 years [1] to go from the 3rd to the 4th level. That's what you and I are now looking at. This is what's called the Great Fall, and the Atlanteans lost far more than just 26,000 years of hard-earned progress.

Recall the consciousness grid plays a role in communicating. It also plays a roll in collective memory (recall the monkeys). Thus they lost that tool as well. They were babies all over again, who knew nothing, were hungry, and did not even know how to build a fire. It was bad.

Thankfully, the priesthood was not affected, because they were safely in the higher dimensions. Thus mommy and daddy were still around, in a sense. But mommy and daddy were beside themselves and had no clue what to do. Just imagine having millions of possessed babies all at once.

7.1 *The 3ʳᵈ Dimension (E note)*

We now have to cover a "piano" topic that we've intentionally delayed until now.

If you look at the piano keys it's rather strange that there is not a black key between the E and F notes. Why are there two white notes in a row? What's going on?

It turns out that inserting this E note is what creates duality consciousness, i.e., it inserts your willpower or ego because you can now operate via your brain (mind) and not just your heart. It creates free will. Thus Lucifer somehow created and inserted this E note. Per Drunvalo [1], we know for sure that the geometries of the 2nd and 4th level consciousness grids are sound designs based on the Fibonacci. However, the 3rd level grid is not. It is way off. That's one of the reasons why we are doing a miserable job taking care of our home - - the Earth. We are not in harmony with it. This is one reason why we seem to take it for granted and thus deplete it.

Thus the Atlanteans were, and likewise we are, stuck on this disharmonious white key. We are destroying Earth. We are destroying all the other species. We are destroying each other.

7.2 *Back to the Great Fall*

Most of you have heard of Murphy's Law. This is Murphy's Law at its best. We not only (1) had the Great Fall, we (2) got stuck on this disharmonious E note; (3) we forgot everything (this is extremely important to realize), and (4) we are still in duality consciousness. Our egos get in the way a lot - - and far more so because we have to struggle so much just to survive. The only people we care about are ourselves and our loved ones. Also don't forget that (5) the culprits (the bad-guys) are still here and still at it, doing everything they can to prevent us from progressing.

Help!!!!

That's exactly what the uppermost priesthood did. They asked for help. They put a corresponding plan together. They got permission (unlike the bad-guys). They've taken action, and here we are now, 13,000 years later, on the brink of being successful.

They, and others, have done a lot. The next chapter explains all of that.

Here, however, realize that this is a rare event in our universe. Now you can understand, even if you find this hard to believe, why 250,000 cultures around our universe are watching these events unfold on Earth. They are glued to their TV sets.

And here we are - - on the brink of the Fibonacci. To do that, we need to understand our past, and the next chapter provides another big piece of that past.

Chapter 8: The Big Fix

Chapter 8

- The Big Fix -

Regarding the Great Fall, notice how much of this is related to Sacred Geometry (and the "piano"). The bad-guys are here in the first place because someone was playing with Sacred Geometry eons ago (an earlier Lucifer-type experiment). Then the stage became Earth, and the bad-guys built a Sacred Geometry tool (the pyramid), and that caused the Great Fall. It destroyed the Consciousness Grid (more geometry), which ruined our collective memory and our ability to ascend.

To fix this, we just couldn't just go to the doctor and take a pill. We couldn't just pray and hope that God would fix it overnight. Reading the Bible or listening to Jimmy Swaggart isn't going to do it either.

This is one of those cases where you really have to pull back the covers on what God really is. The fact that the bad-guys were building a synthetic reality machine, and if they were successful then you and I would be living in that world today, gives you a flavor on just how much the "covers are pulled back".

The good-guys know these technologies as well - - and much more. I'm speaking about the uppermost priesthood, and by that I mean those who are in tune with (and thus from) the upper dimensions (highest piano notes). In these lectures, these are known as the Ascended Masters.

Even if you are a good-guy, you can't just show up here on Earth and start playing around with these Sacred Geometry technologies, much less the piano. You need permission. Recall my proposal that the universe has a QC department. You need permission from the next level up, and that could be, for example, a Solar Council or a Galaxy Council - - consisting of even wiser Ascended Masters. Gordon Asher Davidson in *The Transfiguration of our World* explains that this is exactly the case. The Earth and the other planets are chakras in our solar system body. Beyond that are chakras associated with our galaxy. Beyond that are seven galaxies that comprise an even higher hierarchy chakra level, and so on.

Regardless of whether or not you can accept this hierarchy per se, it makes sense that whatever you do needs to be part of the bigger plan. Thus any repairs have to be harmonious with the larger Sacred Geometry scenario (e.g., the universe itself). Thus even though the universe might be perfect, there are apparently perturbations here and there (such as the mess Earth is in) - - and the necessary levels address it and manifest a collective unity consciousness solution.

8.1 Thoth

The bottom line of the Great Fall is it ruined (or delayed by multiples of 100,000 years) our ability to move up the piano notes, and we need to get that ability back.

With this in mind, I am pleased to introduce you to Thoth.

Thoth has been around 60,000 years or more, since well before the birth of Atlantis. He's obviously learned to become immortal (Immortality is not as big a deal as you may think. We cover this in Chapter 11). He's had several names and, to keep things simple, we'll stick with one of them - - Thoth (rhymes with oath).

Thoth was the "king" of Atlantis during its last 16,000 years. This implies he was of the most spiritually advanced (wisest) and was from the highest level (piano note).

Thoth, Ra Ta, and Araragat were the three (most visible) Ascended Masters who stepped up to the plate and helped us through this catastrophic disaster. Please note these names for future reference.

They were able to somewhat contain the situation, i.e., to repair the consciousness grids of the lower levels and put most of the entities back where they belong [1]. However, the main population "fell" back to very bottom of the 3rd level (the E note) and, in doing so, lost all of the progress that had been achieved. (I have not mentioned this before. Between each note on the piano are twelve mini-notes or overtones. The Atlanteans had achieved a high mini-note level. This progress is what was lost.)

That mass population was still very sick and had no choice but to endure the long-term nightmare, and we are talking 13,000 years -- right up to us today.

8.2 Consciousness Grid Project

Permission was granted [1] to do something highly unusual (in the universe). We were allowed to re-create the 4th level consciousness grid from scratch. That means building a *synthetic* consciousness grid.

That's incredible! Talk about being given the chance to be born again! Normally you can't interfere with consciousness -- populations have to simply grow on their own. However, since we had already achieved a 4th level grid, and were victims of foul play which destroyed it, permission was granted.

However, this meant that we had to build an electromagnetic grid around the entire Earth -- and it has to have 83,000 structures (at intersections points and along gridlines) in order to be a perfect dodecahedron crystal. Then it has to actually work.

Think about it. It's incredible that we are going to create this synthetic grid, much less that someone "above" actually approved the plan. What's also incredible is it's not mentioned in the Bible other than symbolically as part of the Great Fall.

Now imagine that *you* have the job of building this Consciousness Grid. How do you go about it? Briefly stated, Thoth & Co. designed and built the entire grid, but on a higher level of consciousness. That's relatively easy because, on the higher levels, you simply imagine it and it's there. However, think of this thought-manifested-grid as a model, because the real one then has to be built on the 3rd dimension. That's your backyard. Now you have to deal with real and heavy rocks. It's a bit more difficult.

Drunvalo [1] provides a detail explanation of the how the Great Pyramid and neighboring structures were built "through consciousness and in a matter of hours". The location and orientation of those structures involve a pattern of ten Golden Mean spirals (more Sacred Geometry). Surveyors today would have a difficult time making such an alignment. Thoth himself built the single primary structure, which is the Great Pyramid, and he built it from the top down [Link 101]. In that link, Drunvalo had today's Egyptian authorities study the mortar (1990s) and the conclusion was the upper stones were older than the lower stones, i.e., they were placed first. The Egyptians have never shared this information.

In and of itself, the Great Pyramid is an amazing tool with multiple functions. However, regarding the Grid itself, the Great Pyramid is the main reference point. It was literally the reference GPS "home" position. It is located, intentionally, at the center of gravity of the earth-land-mass. As you know, the continents are moving all the time. However, this particular location (being the center of gravity) does not drift. It remains fixed.

After the Great Pyramid was complete (about 13,000 years ago), construction slowly began on the other 83,000 "pyramids" required to complete the grid. All over the world, and at precise GPS coordinates, structures such as Machu Picchu, Stonehenge, and the Inca and Mayan temples were created. Pyramids in Japan, Tibet, as well as constructed hills in Ohio, and even natural phenomena like the Oregon Vortex were all part of this detailed matrix. These were built with hard-core labor. The indigenous tribes were given detailed instructions by their priesthoods including the exact pin-point GPS location. We already mentioned the work of Carl Munck [8] providing astonishing insights, i.e., how the structures readily reveal their own GPS coordinates. Here is a conveniently short video [Link 802] revealing the same.

Finally it was finished. All 83,000 locations were completed by essentially everyday folks toiling for thousand of years. You can now begin to appreciate the indigenous tribes all over the world. The modern world has typically treated them horribly, such as the slaughter of the American Indians, the devastation by the Spanish Conquistadors, the constant bombardment by righteous Christian Missionaries, etc. Yet through it all they have maintained their ancient ways, wisdom, and agenda.

These structures in and of themselves are not the grid. The grid is the electromagnetic pattern these structures create above them, as well as below them, in the Earth. The electromagnetic waves themselves are roughly 1,000 feet (300 meters) in diameter. We can measure these waves, and the government knows all about them.

Like building a car from the parts, the car is now built. There are no more parts on your workbench. However, you don't just go and turn the key. First you have to tune it up. (Incidentally, we have plenty of gas, thanks to the 7.23 cm energy.) That tuning started around 1980.

Notice the date - -1980. That means now. This is not some fairy tale. Thus it's time to sit up in your chair and take notice.

8.3 Why Now?

Before I get into the fine-tuning, I want to share some personal experiences regarding "why now"?

It is well researched that if 1% of a given population does TM (Transcendental Meditation), then that entire population has fewer car accidents, fewer hospital visits, etc.

Close friends of mine were into TM in a major way. This was about 1993, and the Maharishi began teaching an advanced meditation technique call Siddhis (this is not for amateurs as it can be dangerous). Lo and behold, the one friend began levitating, and did so regularly with his local group. They all did. There were twenty three of them. I immediately asked him what he was feeling during these levitations. "Total bliss" was the immediate response. That's unity consciousness at work.

With the new advanced technique, however, only 7,000 people meditating would have the same effect - - on the entire world - - as 1% of the entire world meditating the "old" way. However they have to be meditating at the same place and at the same time. This was coordinated worldwide. There were 7,000 in a certain spot in India, 7,000 more in Amsterdam, and 7,000 more in Iowa (yes.. Iowa), as well as local groups. This coordinated meditation continues today.

To me these things (the levitating and everyone meditating at once) were one thing. But my real question was "*why now*"? Why didn't the TM masters learn and teach these "advanced" techniques 2,000, 1,000, or 500 years ago? Why now? What is so special about now? (Humorously, I wonder if magic carpet rides actually did exist....)

Now, twenty-five years later, I realize that it's likely linked to the grid being complete. It was time to shift into a higher gear, and the Maharishi and thousands of other masters around the world got the message (got permission) and took appropriate action.

8.4 Tuning Up the Grid

One of those actions was the fine-tuning of the grid. These masters, their students, and other spiritually advanced individuals (100,000-150,000 of them) were instructed to place crystals (quartz crystals) at specific locations in and around the 83,000 structures around the world. Roughly a million crystals were placed. Their instructions came to them during meditation [Link 801, Link 101].

This fine-tuned the energy flow pattern of the Grid. This is not some science fiction story. It's exactly like a car. We had to tune it up! There is no difference.

Crystals have special properties. I knew that as a Boy Scout building a crystal radio - - the crystal is what receives the radio signal. The silicon in our computers is a crystal. You can program quartz (silicon dioxide) crystals was well. Thus these individuals programmed the quartz crystals per their given instructions, and then placed them in service. The actual power used to program the crystals is Love, i.e., unity consciousness with clear intention. This is well known technology that goes back to ancient times and far beyond.

Thus 1989 is when the grid was technically tuned up. However, there were still issues.

_____

The next step was to use ceremony to remove things that were blocking the energy flows. Call it therapy if you wish, or removing demons, software issues, or whatever. Like a car that's been assembled, tuned up with instruments, you then turn the key, but it won't start. Thus it's either not getting gas or not getting current to the spark plugs. You need to do a bit of troubleshooting.

These were tribal issues, as opposed to structural issues. Indigenous tribes around the world are linked to our distant past. That's pretty much defines the word indigenous, i.e., their history goes way back tens of thousand of years.

In some cases, these ceremonies were simply due diligence due to the grid being complete. In other cases, some of these tribes had also terribly sinned - - the result of the Great Fall and the chaos and confusion that followed. In the worst case it was things like cannibalism or human sacrifice. Ceremonies were needed to repent and clear the blockages (karma).

These ceremonies, all of them, are where Drunvalo really becomes a key player, along with roughly fifty, or so, other key individuals from all over the world [Link 201, Link 101] who are likewise linked with the Ascended Masters. They were from all religious backgrounds, including Christianity, as well as the indigenous tribes. Drunvalo & Co. were invited (remember you need permission). They never asked to go to these places, but instead were invited "out of the blue". (Again my good question is "Why now?" Why did numerous tribes invite them now, and invite them independently of the other tribes?)

Furthermore, this group of advanced individuals had to prove to the indigenous tribes that they were in full contact with Mother Earth. Thus eagles magically still (levitating) a few feet directly overhead [Link 201] for ten minutes, and the like, were signs that the indigenous tribes needed to prove to themselves that Drunvalo & Co. were the real deal. As you'll learn, Mother Earth is far more than just dirt under your feet.

Likewise, the ceremony was not just show up, stand up, sit down, build a fire, dance a little, and be done with it. The ceremonies were as magical to the visitors as they were to the indigenous people. A big part of these ceremonies is connecting with "Mother Earth and Father Sky". "Mother Earth" is just that, recognizing that she is our Mother (we came from her) and is very much alive and has a chakra system just like us. "Father Sky" represents everything else, i.e., all life everywhere here and in the cosmos, and this includes the moon, sun, planets, galaxies, etc.

Drunvalo & Co. passed all these tests with flying colors and likewise the ceremonies were greatly successful, and let's just say that's an understatement. Many of these had not been performed in 13,000 years, and their time was due again - - now. They were completed. They could not have been done without the modern world (Drunvalo & Co.) present with the ancient world. Tears of joy poured from all once they realized what had been finally achieved [Link 201]. Magical "thank you" responses occurred from both Mother Earth and Father Sky. In one case a beam of light came down from above. In the final case, a star-shaped emblem (Light) appeared and remained on the beach for several days. Also, the beautiful fish returned to the (otherwise dead) reef a few days later.

Timing-wise, the crystals were in place in 1985. The first due diligence ceremonies took place in 1987, the repenting-oriented ones were thereafter, and the last was a due diligence ceremony performed in Tahiti in 2008.

That's *twenty-five* years of coordinated effort, and ceremonies with Drunvalo & Co. (representing the modern world) and the indigenous tribes (the ancient world). You have a lot of thanking to do. These ceremonies invariably included a specific pattern on the ground, made with rocks, flowers, candles, etc. Those patterns reflect Sacred Geometry.

February 2008 is when we made it. The Grid is complete and working. It is just a waiting game now.

8.5 Airplane Analogy (Intro)

It is just a waiting game was mentioned just above, and if you were actually paying attention, you'd be asking, "Waiting for *what?*"

That is what the next few chapters, in fact all of them, are about. We've been waiting on, or working on, one thing or another for 13,000 years since the Great Fall. The Grid (the Big Fix) is just one piece (although a big one) of that waiting game.

Time, in and of itself, is another piece. We'll cover that in the next chapter.

Another huge piece, however, is you and me. We have to get our act together in order to get onto the new grid. All these events are leading the horse to water, but the horse itself has to ultimately drink. That's you and me. No one is going to wave a magic wand, and that includes Jesus or God. That's the Cinderella complex. Life just doesn't work that way. Free will is required, and it's all about the math.

Recall from Chapter 2 that the "math" is a Fibonacci event which includes you and me as participants. Everything grows in finite steps in accordance with the Fibonacci. That includes mass consciousness growth (graduating to a higher level).

Thus, the question is "how do we get properly aligned" for this Fibonacci event of getting onto the new Grid? What counts? You washing the dishes and me mowing the lawn are not the answer. Going to church and throwing money in a collection plate won't work either. Neither will listening to Jimmy Swaggart.

With that new grid comes the new dimension - - the 4th Level. However, it is not a freebie. We have to make it happen.

The Grid being complete is like a big airplane parked at the gate, and mechanically ready to take off (take us to Heaven and be with Jesus - - if you prefer those words).

Thus, to help us through the following chapters, I'm going to use the analogy of an airplane that's about to take off.

Here is the checklist for Getting Aligned:

One of the first things is to get rid of our luggage, i.e., get rid of our egos. It's intuitively obvious that we need to be in unity consciousness as best we can. Jesus taught this, as do all religions and spiritual teachers. We know the recipe. We just have to do it.

If we were all levitating in our living rooms, there would be no reason to write these lectures. We'd be perfectly aligned.

This may very well have been the case had the Great Fall not occurred. Levitating is simply a symptom of pure bliss, i.e., pure unity consciousness - - like an eagle floating stationary over your head. So are all the miracles that Jesus performed. There are plenty of other symptoms.

The problem is the Great Fall did occur, we are not of unity consciousness, and each and every one of us has to do the best we can. Thus we have to get rid of our luggage, get in our seats next to one another, and then get aligned.

The captain is waiting for the appropriate OK from the flight attendants.

The captain is also waiting for the appropriate OK from the control tower.

We will take off when both of these are OK. That is when we are fully aligned.

With this in mind, let's now begin the rest of these lectures.

Chapter 9

- Time (The Seasons) -

Having the new consciousness grid up and running is one thing but, as described by the airplane analogy, getting ourselves on it and fully operating is the next major challenge.

The basic challenge is we forgot everything. We've forgotten our history. We've forgotten our hearts. We've forgotten how to grow and move up the piano notes.

Thoth and others who followed were well aware of this problem and took steps to help us remember.

Just imagine having a bunch of junior high kids (that's about how advanced we were on fully achieving the 4th dimension when the Great Fall occurred) and having to keep them up to speed (and their children, and their children's children, for countless generations). It's a daunting task. Remember, also, that whatever they did required permission, and they could not interfere directly (like plugging us in and automatically programming us). They could only "encourage" us to learn. We have to make the commitment and actually do it ourselves - - individually. That's free will.

How long is the school year for these kids? We had the Great Fall. How long do we have to fix things? Is there is a timeline?

The answer to all these questions is yes. We have a deadline!

In our Sacred Geometry discussions thus far, I never mentioned time. What's the deal? DNA doesn't know time. Pyramids don't know time. God doesn't use a stopwatch. Nonetheless it turns out that there definitely is a timing issue.

For the airplane analogy, you can think of this timing issue as "catching the wind at the right moment". Planes head into the wind when they take off. Thus just imagine a high wind that is constantly changing direction, yet in a very predictable rotating manner. You have to time things so the plane takes off going into the wind, and then you really start making time (after you are airborne) when that wind finally gets behind you. We need both!

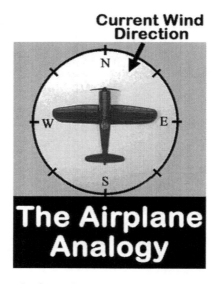

Thus, we have get rid of our luggage, get our seat belts fastened, etc., and be ready just in time as the wind rotates in our favor for takeoff.

9.1 *The Timeline (Seasons)*

When we talk "time" in Sacred Geometry, we are really talking about seasonal cycles.

We have the days (one Earth rotation), the months (one moon rotation around the Earth), the seasons (one Earth rotation around the sun), and the next cycle in this sequence (which we don't pay attention to because it's twenty-six thousand years long...) is the one that applies to the grid. It is called the Precession of the Equinox. It's a long name, and perhaps has a castor oil flavor to it for some, but it's really nothing more than just the next "season" beyond the ones we are readily familiar with. Beyond that are other important cycles, and one of those, related to the magnetic pole shift, is about 2.1 million years. That one is in the news!

From a Sacred Geometry (and Piano) viewpoint, these cycles or seasons are really nothing more than sine waves - - just like the vibrating strings of the piano or a guitar.

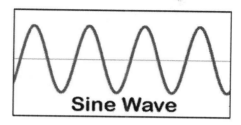

You can think of "time", therefore, as the distance between the peaks. This distance is 24 hours for a day, 720 hours (30 days x 24) for a month, etc. Jesus, Thoth, and virtually everyone we talk about were very familiar with the Precession of the Equinox. It takes 26,000 years for a complete cycle. This is shown by the sine wave below.

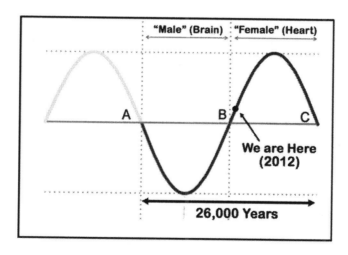

Figure 9-2. The Precession of the Equinox, like all seasons, is a sine wave. Its Frequency (Wavelength) is 26,000 years.

Notice it dips down, and then it goes high again. From Point A to Point C is one complete cycle. That's 26,000 years, and we are back to where we started, and then it repeats again and again. These sine waves always have a plus and minus associated with them. When you are above the horizontal line it's "plus", and when you are below, it's "minus". You can relate this to the daily darkness and light cycle, to our annual temperature swings, to the phases of the moon and tides, etc.

9.2 Male versus Female Cycle

Notice, also, that the first half of the cycle is "male" and the second half is "female" [Link 1501].

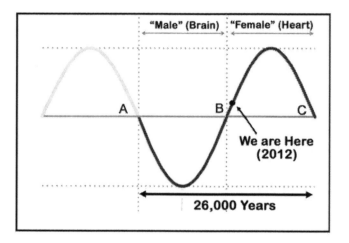

This is very important to understand.

Please realize that there is no single word (word-pair) in the English language to describe "male" versus "female". This is not about human males and females. That's the reason for the quotation marks. Truer word-pairs would be electric versus magnetic, and logic versus pure consciousness. There are other pairs as well. However, the convention is to use "male" versus "female" to collectively represent all of these word-pairs.

We'll first give you the actual *physics* of the situation:

When you run current through a wire, you get both an electrical field and a matching magnetic field. They are a matched pair - - just like plus/minus, night/day, etc. The "male" portion is the electrical, and the "female" portion is the magnetic. The electrical is in the wire itself. It is very defined - - similar to the straight lines in Metatron's cube. The magnetic field is like an aura. It surrounds the wires, and thus is not as defined - - like the circles in The Flower of Life.

What does this mean in everyday terms? For 13,000 years we think via the brain (mind), and for the next 13,000 years we think via pure consciousness (the heart). Pure consciousness can create those miraculous, almost instantaneous healings. This is the "female" at work. Such miraculous healings don't make sense to the "male". The "male" dominated by logic and thinks about the discrete pieces of the puzzle and how they fit together. They'd rather build logical instruments with which to do the healings.

It may seem crazy that our brains are impacted by traveling around the universe, but think about this: it's rather crazy that we sleep for eight hours a day, not to mention that we have dreams. We also have biorhythm cycles. These behaviors alert you that we are more than just a robot that goes to work every day. We are electronically connected to what's "out there" somehow, and we interact with that. We are part of it, and vice versa. Our life and our entire reality are comprised of a bunch of cycles.

Atlantis had just ended 13,000 years of "female", and this is why they were successful in making rapid spiritual progress. It's far easier to obtain unity consciousness in a "female" cycle. Unity consciousness is love for all and everything.

Thus Atlantis was doing just fine, and when the Great Fall occurred, it coincided with us entering the "male" cycle. Unity consciousness (living via the heart) took a back seat in favor of the mind. This is yet another Murphy's Law item (in addition to the bad-guys, the duality consciousness, and the Great Fall) all happening at once. Now we have some exaggerated egos in the general population mix - - not to mention a nonstop tradition of greed and war.

Help!!

But now, after 13,000 years of waiting and preparations, 2012 is the end of that "male" cycle, and things are *finally* turning around.

9.3 Being Asleep vs. Awake

In addition to "male" versus "female" aspect, there's another cycle superimposed on the Precession of the Equinox. It involves how awake or asleep our consciousness is [1]. It's like having the temperature swings of summer versus winter, yet also having a rainy and dry season superimposed on that.

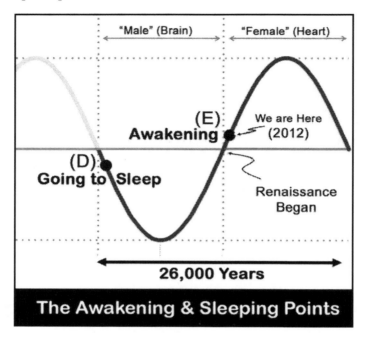

Figure 9-3. The Awakening and Sleeping Points on the Precession of the Equinox

The location of going to sleep, and especially that of waking up, is of paramount importance. Thankfully, Murphy's Law is finally in our favor again! These awakening & sleeping points are shown above by the dark dots.

Point D above is when we fell asleep. That's right after the Great Fall, about the time that Atlantis sank. It was 13,000 years ago, and we've slept until now.

The next couple of chapters cover the events during this "sleepy male" period, when Thoth & Co. were trying to keep things together as best they could.

That's because they were anticipating Point E.

That's when we start waking up! That's what the Mayan Calendar was all about. Thus 2012 was simply the alarm clock telling us it's time to wake up, do the ceremonies, etc. We can now confess that several of

Drunvalo & Co.'s ceremonies were tied to this awakening moment, i.e., tied specifically to the Precession of the Equinox. The Mayans (of Central America) are well known as the "keepers of time", and those ceremonies were indeed initiated by them. Those ceremonies had not been done for 13,000 years!

It is no coincidence that the Grid completion was timed with this awakening moment. That was planned 13,000 years ago. It is no coincidence that people started levitating in the 1980s. They were finally waking up after 13,000 years!

This is why everyone has a sense of "something's going on" or "something's about to happen." We are waking up! We are also becoming more and more "female". The Grid is complete and some of us are communicating with it. That's three Murphy's Laws that are becoming undone. The tables are finally turning in our favor. Amen!

For the airplane analogy, it's getting easier by the minute for us to "Get Aligned".

9.4 How Much Time do We Have?

As far as the airplane analogy goes, the wind is definitely headed in right direction for take-off as I write this, and the captain is anxiously waiting the all-clear signal from the flight attendants.

We are exactly where we need to be - - right now. Timing-wise, this is what 2012 is about. We are at the right place (the Precession of the Equinox) at the right time (the Awakening Female). We just need to Get Aligned.

The Big Bang and a Universe from Nothing

Recall our "A Universe from Nothing" discussion from Chapter 1. From nothing, you can get a sine wave. Thus you suddenly have a plus and a minus, where before you had nothing.

Physicists acknowledge that there's matter and anti-matter, energy and dark energy, etc. Along with this is the realization that the darkness (in the night sky) is just as important as the light (the stars, etc.). These are nothing more than the plus and minus humps of a sine wave. It's that "simple".

Now, perhaps, you can at least get a glimpse of the Big Bang. From "Nothing" you can create a sine wave. You then have something.

Spirit scientists recognize there is the "Great Void" and then there is "Nothing". These are quite different. The Great Void, in which (space-wise) God created everything, is indeed nothing (that means zip, nothing, naught). Within that void he then used "Nothing" (the prana) to create everything.

Perhaps this allows you to grasp what God did in Genesis. Within the Great Void, from the "Nothing" (prana) came the sine waves, and these sine waves then manifested into everything we know, including time, i.e., all the cycles mentioned above. Simply think of time as a sine wave.

Not only time, but space also manifested. You've heard of Einstein's space-time continuum. Now you are an expert in relativity! Don't forget the 7.23 cm energy. It appeared as well, and Einstein put a number on it of 10^{96} (See Chapter 1).

Note the challenge the Bible-writer had in attempting to relate this information to the sleeping masses, back in the age when making sandals from dead animals was considered high-technology. What would you have written?

9.5 *Male versus Female (Again)*

The entire discussion above is a very "male". It laboriously goes step by step, and there's plenty of head scratching to do until you are comfortable. That's because physics is a very "male" subject (Please recall that we are not talking about the human sexes).

The "female" version is that simply that "God created the Heavens and the Earth". He used this heart. It was pure consciousness. It was simple.

This is what the Precession of the Equinox is all about. This is what 2012 is about. Logic is departing us in favor of miracles (prana and consciousness) instead.

Now, speaking of the actual human sexes, women (and children) are going to have a much easier time making the 2012 transition. You may not believe me, but we are going to clean up Mother Earth, and make her the beautiful place she once was, using only our consciousness. Women, naturally, are more gifted in this arena.

I can say this with 100% confidence because there are meditations that are very "female" (using your heart), and men typically have a difficult time with it. Instructors invariably have to come up with a much more logical, lengthy, step by step meditation so that the men can hopefully catch up. It is always a challenge. We'll discuss these meditations briefly in Chapter 15, and provide links.

9.6 The "Timing" of Jesus

Do you think the arrival of Jesus on the scene (his timing) was a random event?

The arrival of Jesus, and his emphasizing the "female" way, is very much in sync with this cycle. He taught consciousness and created miracles. He did not teach physics.

We were dead asleep, and like catching a plane first thing in the morning, something needed to be our alarm clock and wake us up, so that we can at least eat and start heading to the airport.

Was that the intention of Jesus?

The next chapter addresses this timing of Jesus and other landmark events.

Note that 2012, by contrast, is the alarm clock for the plane to actually take off. We address this date head-on in Chapter 15 "Getting Aligned".

Chapter 10

-More Fixes (The Classroom)-

The new consciousness grid is up and running. However the population needs to be awakened, educated, and in alignment before we "take off". The basic challenge is we forgot everything. We've forgotten our history. We've forgotten Sacred Geometry. We've forgotten our hearts. We've forgotten how to grow and move up the piano notes.

Thoth, and others who followed, were well aware of this problem and took steps to help us remember. Here are the major school "classes" that we took over the course of the 13,000 years. These are presented both in graphic form (the sine wave) and in a table.

The Great Fall occurred roughly 13,000 years ago. Thoth built the Great Pyramid about 200 years later. Soon after construction began all over the world on the 83,000 structures, and continued for thousands of years. After that began the real "Classroom" events we cover in this chapter.

The Major Events

10.1 Sumer and Egypt

About 5,500 years ago, or roughly 3,500 B.C., the first blatant "classroom" event occurred. The Egyptian and Sumerian cultures were proactively cultivated. As far as "school" goes, these cultures were fed information at a rate they could handle and use. These Ascended Masters (just like parents or Montessori school teachers) would simply watch the population, and when they saw a person or a pocket of people who were ready to take on a new level of awareness, they'd appear as normal people and feed them the appropriate information.

Sumer was located in Mesopotamia, between the Tigris and Euphrates rivers, in current day Iraq. Egypt recognized the power of the "female", yet was also a "male" culture. This is why you see Egyptian drawings showing men with all kinds of weird "tools", usually sticking out of the rear of their necks. They were aware of the Great Fall and were attempting to *synthetically* reconnect themselves to the higher levels.

For those who were ready, the Great Pyramid itself was the ultimate place to go because you could actually ascend to the higher levels. Pyramids are well known to concentrate energy. Today people meditate while sitting under stick-pyramids to have an enhanced experience. Within the Great Pyramid, the king's chamber and queen's chamber, and all the corresponding tunnels, are designed in a very specific Sacred Geometry pattern [1] - - specifically for this ascension process. You would actually "go to Heaven" and then come back. It was practice for the real thing.

Years Ago	Major Event	Date
13,000	- The Great Fall	11,000 B.C.
12,800	- Thoth created the Great Pyramid - Atlantis Sank	10,800 B.C.
5,500	- Egypt and Sumer were born. - Sumer began stepwise evolution. - Egyptians Practiced Ascension in Great Pyramid.	3300 B.C.
3500	- Akhenaton emphasized single God. - Akhenaton's work ultimately led to the Essene Brotherhood. - He ruled only 17 years.	1500 B.C.
2500	- The Essene Brotherhood was born, anticipating Jesus. - Greece, and its "Religion of Math", was borne. - The Druid "Religion of the Earth" was born in England. - Buddha was born in Tibet.	500 B.C.
2000	- Jesus and the Essenes (We were dead asleep)	0
25	- Consciousness Grid Completed (Structural)	1989
6	- Grid Tuned Up & Turned on. - All "2012" ceremonies completed.	2008

But the population overall was still asleep, so success was mediocre at best. Imagine teaching a class of sleepy students. As a result, things declined and got very confusing over time. The Egyptians were aware of the 42 + 2 chromosomes in our DNA, and this resulted in 44 such "gods". Recall, just like a teacher, all the Masters could do was feed them information and then stand back and watch. It became a real mess.

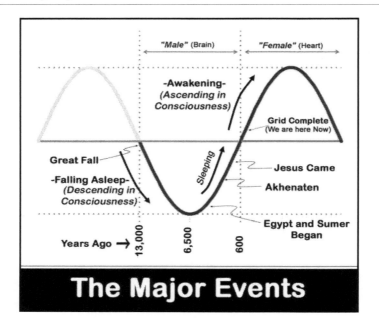

The Major Events

10.2 *Akhenaten & the First Immortals*

Thus Thoth & Co. had to do something dramatic. They did. Thoth walked into the room of the current king of Egypt at the time and "convinced" him (Amenhotep II) not have his son be the next king, but rather let Thoth install the next king. I presume Amenhotep was in awe that someone like Thoth was in this presence. Imagine Jesus walking into your room and asking you the same question. "No problem" says the king.

Thus Akhenaten eventually became the king of Egypt. This was about 3,500 years ago, or about 1,500 B.C. Akhenaten was intentionally "created" as a 4th level being, 14 feet tall with a large head (so he's quite intelligent). He became the first Pharaoh, which means "that which you will become". His father actually ruled before him and thus paved the way for his son to be king. Since he was a 4th level being, he ruled from the heart. He was not a tyrant or anything of the sort.

The statues of him indeed reflect a 14-ft being. He made radical changes and was killed after just 17 years of rule. You can't really "kill" 4th dimensional beings, so there is some mystery around what exactly happened to him. Perhaps he decided it was time to "move on up". Who knows? (FYI, per some scholars, his son and successor was the young king Tut.)

Nonetheless, we might not be here today, and especially tomorrow, if it were not for Akhenaten. He quickly got rid of all the "gods" and replaced them with a single thing to worship - - the Sun. He was fully aware that the Sun was a makeshift god analogy, but it suited the needs for the time. He's also famous for eliminating the traditional Egyptian art and replacing it with actual "true" pictures of plants and animals. He also got rid of clothing, so everyone walked around virtually nude. His whole philosophy was about being "true" to yourself and others, having just the one God, and recognizing that the one God is accessible within yourself, i.e., you don't need priests or anyone else to access God.

More importantly, Akhenaten created the Egyptian Mystery School. The school was twelve physical structures, and each structure was associated with one of the twelve chakras. You'd spend a year or more in each school. These were serious schools, and it was not just an issue of going through the motions. In the first one, for example, you'd swim in the presence of huge alligators to help you overcome any emotional fears you might have. You graduated that school once you overcame all your fears.

Far more important than the school itself was about 300 of Akhenaten's students successfully achieved immortality [1]. They graduated into the "final classroom" - - the Great Pyramid - - and in there, they were successful in dying (ascending) and coming back.

Although Akhenaten was killed by Egyptians, i.e., the priesthood who saw their powers being stripped away, these 300 immortals (both men and women) went on to do great things. They were the first immortals from Earth (homo-sapiens) other than maybe one or two produced early-on in the Lemurian days.

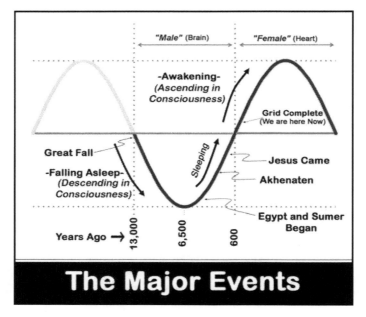

The Major Events

Let's go back to the sine wave (above) and review the timeline. All of these events we've covered are between the low-spot (6,500 years ago) and where we are now (Grid complete). First was the Egyptian and Sumerian cultures, then Akhenaten a couple thousand years later, and then Jesus fifteen hundred years after that. All of this is during the "sleeping male" period. During this entire period the 83,000 structures were being built all over the world by indigenous tribes whose spiritual leaders are getting instructions "from above".

10.3 Jesus

This brings us to the subject of Jesus himself. We'll cover Jesus in great depth in the next two chapters.

Jesus arrived when the "male" 13,000 year cycle was 85% complete (2000 years ago).

Akhenaten and Jesus had the same basic philosophy. There is but one God, and it's available within you (no church or other party required). It's an all-powerful God, and you can tap that power provided you are truthful and learn how (through unity consciousness and intention). Ultimately you can resurrect (ascend) to Heaven (the higher notes) and have everlasting life (be immortal). The latter terms (those in parentheses) are Akhenaten's.

Akhenaten had his Mystery School and taught there. His students came when he called.

Jesus, on the other hand, walked around barefoot from town to town and used his only tool - - his body. He had to perform - - literally - - and make a huge impression wherever he went. He certainly did!

Regarding 2012, his mission was the same as everyone else - - to help us undo the Great Fall and get back on track. It's intuitively obvious that Jesus knew about 2012. He taught consciousness.

10.4 Others

Jesus taught unity consciousness and for us to aware of the pitfalls of duality consciousness. Akhenaten and Jesus both taught the one God.

However, these events occurred 2,000 to 4,000 of years ago. We need a refresher course. We need to know more than this to get through 2012, such as our true history, and we also need more people who can demonstrate (as teachers) such skills. There have been many who have come to help us through this transition, right up to today. In this section, however, we are going to cover how this occurs. How do they come?

Recall the piano:

**Akhenaten Populated
The Higher Notes (for Us)**

All the white keys on the piano are now occupied. This is what Akhenaten achieved. He ran the fish hatchery, so to speak, and stocked our creek with the first 300 immortals (following the Great Fall). Those, in turn, are helping others do the same. That's you and me. The problem is - - we're stuck on the 3rd note (E note), yet those teachers are now on the 4th level and above. There's even more on the higher levels, and even beyond, and thus much wiser beings that were not caught in the Great Fall. They've been helping us all along as well.

So how can they teach us anything? How can the agenda items (such as building the 83,000 structures) actually get designed and properly built by everyday people? Even today, we need to get through the Fibonacci. How can they help us with that? How does this communication occur?

Those are the questions, and here are the answers. Here are different ways that help can, and does, occur.

The first way is they actually come to the 3rd level. Their electrical body (their chakra system) comes and their soul is right there accompanying it. If it helps, think of the soul as the magnetic field which always accompanies the electric field. They are born into a regular human body. However, since they are from the higher levels, they have a much easier time being in unity consciousness. This means they are more in contact with their heart, as opposed to just using their brain (mind). That might come in handy during our required Fibonacci event. They can also more easily learn and do miracle healings and other such things that depend on pure consciousness (using the prana).

Second, they can come as teachers. There are many outstanding spiritual teachers. Examples are Ghandi, the Dalai Lama, the Maharishi, as well all the advanced shamans in indigenous cultures. When they look for the next Dalai Lama, they search the Himalayas for the single child that has the most advanced soul, and who demonstrates such. There are also teachers who are not as advanced as these more glorious types. Regardless, all of these teachers use meditation as the venue to obtain further knowledge, and at times, actual instructions. Such is the case with, for example, placing the crystals at the appropriate points on the Consciousness Grid in the 1980s, or the actual building of the Grid itself over the past 13,000 years.

Similar to what's above is the third group. They don't actually come, but instead communicate with someone who previously did. The 5th level (G note) is the highest level on which there is a physical body as we know it. After that it is just thought. These are very wise beings who no longer need or want that physical body because they rely on pure consciousness. They communicate via pure consciousness. This is what telepathic communication is. It's not channeling. In the ideal situation, where both sides are at the top of their game, it's me providing you the entire dictionary in a few seconds. However, normally the lower-level person is not that skilled. I've know a specific case where images were used instead [1]. I know of another case where the conversation is just like you and me conversing today. Such requires decades of training and commitment [5]. I tend to separate this third group from the second via the following: in the second group, the lower ones are the ones initiating the contact (for example, asking a question). The third group would be the higher level beings wanting to proactively get a message out.

Finally, and perhaps the rarest of cases, would be such an advanced individual actually showing up in person. They may manifest as an everyday human or even manifest as an Angel or the like. Hermes is a great example. In the Emerald Tablets [4], Thoth reveals that he showed up as Hermes in ancient Greece (approx 500 B.C.) and taught Sacred Geometry to Pythagoras, bringing him to Egypt as part of those teachings. This launched modern mathematics. Edgar Cayce [9] met an Angel in the forest near his home as a child. He answered her question by stating he wanted to help as many people as possible, especially children. The rest is history. He properly diagnosed 14,000 medical cases, making only one mistake - - he diagnosed one twin instead of the other. Thus, not only did he meet an Angel, he obviously was connected somehow to make these diagnoses. We'll discuss that connection in Chapter 13. There are many Angel stories in the Bible, etc. Likewise, there are countless stories, right up to today, of people meeting strangers who magically showed up at just the right moment to save lives or prevent disasters - - and then disappeared.

10.5 Drunvalo Melchizedek

One such individual, from the second group above, is Drunvalo Melchizedek. A lot of the information in these chapters is from his book *The Ancient Secrets of the Flower of Life.* Please read that book (it's actually two books of 250 pages each, 8 ½ x 11 inch pages.) to understand his background more so. Education-wise he almost got a degree in physics, quitting just before his final quarter and switching to art history. Physics did not have the answers he sought. Art history did. He then spent 25 years learning from spiritual teachers worldwide, very much including the indigenous tribes, to learn and accept their belief systems. He actively participated in their meditations and ceremonies, and they realized that he was something special as well.

He was well aware of 2012 and realized that you and I don't have 40 years (as is the case in Buddhist schools, etc.) to learn the required advanced meditations and get results. That's because we only had a few years before 2012. He therefore condensed that knowledge into brief classes, so that the general population, and especially those of the first and second groups above, can successfully carry out the Fibonacci.

Mathematically a few advanced meditators (i.e., a tiny fraction of the seven billion people on Earth today) can carry the load for the rest of us - - achieving the required Fibonacci. (PS - - that does not mean that you and I can sit back and do nothing. That is the reason for this book.)

Of course, I do not want to take any credit away from the thousands of other teachers worldwide, who have successfully dedicated their lives to achieving this same end.

Another accomplishment of Drunvalo is Sacred Geometry. Although Pythagoras taught it, as usual we forgot it. It was essentially unknown in today's world until Drunvalo came along. It's a huge part of his 500 page book, first published in 1990. Now, twenty-five years later, that Sacred Geometry knowledge has spread worldwide, and has launched a whole new era of technology. How did he get this knowledge? Please read his book to understand, and give merit to, the full story. I'll just say that "Hermes showed up again and taught him". Hermes (Thoth) insisted that Drunvalo, just like Pythagoras, travel to Egypt. This allowed Drunvalo to get all the missing pieces regarding Egypt. We now know that Egypt was a major part of our history and, among other things, that Thoth was there taking notes the whole time - - to get yet wiser and wiser about human behavior.

Finally, Drunvalo was the key person to coordinate finalizing the Consciousness Grid, i.e., to do the final ceremonial necessities to actually turn it on. We'll cover these more so in Chapter 15. This required coordination between the indigenous tribes (our past) with the present (his group of advanced souls from the modern cultures of the word).

Overall, whether or not you accept all of these parts, this is a fascinating story. All my life, just like most of you, I wanted to know the truth of why we are here and exactly what and who we are. One of my big problems was Egypt. How did Egypt, with the pyramids and all those weird figures, mesh with the Bible? What I was getting from books, movies, and those around me was of no help. Egypt appeared extremely advanced, yet was either ignored or simply listed as one of the "Seven Wonders of the World". Everyone just accepted it as an unknown.

Finally I read Drunvalo's "Ancient Secrets of the Flower of Life [1]", and there were the answers I needed, along with the history of Atlantis. It's all there - - hook, line, and sinker. Furthermore, the reason Drunvalo has this knowledge is because Thoth communicated with him for about 10 years (in meditation) starting in 1984. Not only that, Thoth made him go to Egypt and other places. This is exactly what Hermes did to Pythagoras.

Again my question (among others) is "Why now?" The answer is simple. The grid is complete and it's time to get on it. Thoth saw another opportunity, just like he (and others) did in early Egypt and Sumer, and simply "popped up" to make another step-change in our knowledge. He communicated directly with Drunvalo. Drunvalo has since created about 225 teachers, all around the world, to help us better prepare for the grid. He was also very instrumental in tuning it up, as we've discussed.

Drunvalo's own personal history is fascinating in and of itself. He came here from the 7th dimension (12th chromatic level). At age seven, he simply took over someone else's body, with permission of course. He simply got to work. A pair of Angels (his own) has been constantly with him since college, providing instructions on where to go, giving him permission to do this and that, and telling him what he can't do as well.

He knew nothing about life here on Earth and had to learn it all from scratch. Thus he visited and learned from about 72 different indigenous cultures and tribes around the world over two decades. He communicated directly with Thoth and others. This enabled him to put all the pieces together of our history, our future, and much more.

In my opinion his big accomplishments are tuning the grid, making us aware of it and our true history, creating his 225 teachers so they can teach the more advanced souls on this planet what to do at the right times. Very arguably, a most important goal is to get the males "onboard". We are talking real men in this case. Whereas Jesus brought a predominantly "female" approach to teaching, Drunvalo has emphasized the "male" way, intentionally, to reach the hard-to-reach male population.

10.6 Current State

In all the cases we've covered (Egypt, Sumer, Akhenaten, and Jesus) the mass population was still very much asleep. Thus, in Jesus' case as well, maybe a few folks got the message, but the mass population never retained the message and things just degraded - - as usual. That is the state we are in now. We have numerous different religions, factions within those religions, including wars. People look at you funny when you talk about consciousness.

Thus it certainly seems like we need another booster shot - - and like now! After all, it's been 2000 years since Jesus. The good news is we are finally waking up after our 13,000 year nap.

It seems to me one of our latest "booster shots" is the incredible advances in technology over the past 100 years or so. It is not the technology, but rather what it has enabled us to do. It's helping us get aligned.

Here are just a few examples.

There's the web itself. Information goes worldwide in a few seconds. You can make and post your own movie in an hour about any topic you choose, including ascension. As a result the bad-guys (who I've intentionally kept quiet about) are loosing their grip, and they know it.

Other technologies have blossomed the discovery of many ancient civilizations and records, the world's geological history, not to mention outer space, star formation, and black holes. These help reveals the real relevant history of us, as it relates to 2012.

Now there's string theory, and it's leading physicists and spiritual science to the same conclusion regarding what "its" all about - - Sacred Geometry and the piano. The advances in DNA are incredible. That, too, is recognized as Sacred Geometry. It's also changing our views on evolution and where life comes from. It's likewise bringing scientists, spiritual science, and the Bible together.

There's also cutting edge heart-technology, where we can actually measure the toroidal electromagnetic fields around the heart itself, within the heart, and around the body. These are the things that help create "miracles". These are part of Jesus' miracle tool kit. They are also part of the ascension tool kit (everlasting life).

All this technology we are learning is no accident. We are getting lots of help. It does not matter from who or where.

The question, once again, is "Why now?"

My answer is, now that we are starting to wake up, people like Jesus, Thoth, etc., are doing everything they can to reach every possible person in every possible way.

Psychic phenomena are also becoming more and more mainstream. Kids perform miracles all the time. My daughter just bought a special knife to cut vegetables where she baby sits. That six year-old showed her a crayon picture of the exact knife – orange handle and all - - when she showed up:

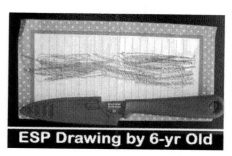

ESP Drawing by 6-yr Old

We simple say "that's weird" and then forget it. Such "miracles" will become commonplace. We are the weird ones by calling *it* "weird". Regardless of what you want to call it, it's helping us, and at times seemingly forcing us, to get aligned. It's a lot like cattle being herded. We're the cattle.

We have a timeline to meet. That is how this chapter began.

Yes, there are predictions of specific events such as Revelations, pole shifts, etc. Many seem to thirst for such specifics, whereas others love them because they can use their ego to criticize them. Such specifics are the "male" way. It's the mind at work. However, it's the "female" that rules. It's the heart that rules. The heart knows no specifics. It just creates.

All we know is that, from a "male" perspective, everything is ready and we are simply waiting on the "female" to act. That's you and me. The bad-guys will simply crumble away as a result. We know that consciousness growth is a Fibonacci event, and this is staring us in the face. This is why we are emphasizing "Getting Aligned".

Time is of the essence.

Thank You !

Tom Price

- Getting Aligned -
For the Planetary Transformation

Part III:
The Melchizedek Files

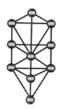

Chapter 11

-The Wise Men (& Women)-

As stated in the prior chapter, Egypt was always on my mind throughout my life as an unanswered question. Once that got answered, which was very recently, the next question became the Wise Men. Who were these guys? They rode camels one thousand miles on a hunch? They followed a star? What's *that* all about?

Then there's John the Baptist. Who was he? How did he know that Jesus was just a few blocks behind him? What's the deal with the water? What's baptism, anyway?

Sure you can take this on pure faith and religious fervor, but when it comes right down to it, these were just everyday people like you and me. Some of the early prophets (Elijah) indeed had "divine intervention", i.e., an advanced sole or Angel from the heavens communicated with them in their sleep, meditation, or broad daylight. However, the Wise Men and John the Baptist did not, as far as I know. This makes my questions that much more enticing.

Edgar Cayce [Link 1103] provides tremendous insights into Jesus and the people surrounding him. Cayce provides fascinating insights into Judy who trained Jesus, Josie who cared for him, Herod and his rages, associated Romans, Jesus himself, his siblings, as well as the Wise Men, John the Baptist and much more.

Cayce did, and continues to do, a tremendous amount of good to help us understand our world including Biblical events. He worked himself to death helping others. At the end of this chapter I'll explain how Cayce "worked". For now, however, I want to focus on the insights from him revealing what happened in the years just prior to, and during, the birth of Jesus.

11.1 The Essenes

[Link 1101, Link 1102] The Essenes were one of three Jewish sects present in the area around the time of Jesus, but they were quite different from the others. The Essenes wrote the Dead Sea Scrolls, and this was during the century immediately before the birth of Jesus. The scrolls were found in 1946 near Qumran (at southern end of the Jordon River), and they were in Egyptian-type containers. Note that the first such scroll was discovered in an Egyptian synagogue in 1897 (50 years prior). The Essenes were also highly influenced by their (the Jewish) earlier exile to Persia.

But there is far more to this Essene story. Edgar Cayce's readings, such as this one provide deeper insights.

- - - - Edgar Cayce 5749:8 - - - -

"In those days when there had been more and more of the leaders of the peoples in Carmel – the original place where the school of prophets was established during Elijah's time."

- - - - - - - -

Elijah is often referred to as the original prophet, and he was around 800 - 900 B.C. Per Cayce he started the School of Prophets, most likely at Mt. Carmel, which is along the coast of (modern day) Israel and near the northern end of the Jordon River.

As is usual in our history, things work for awhile and then we forget and things decline. The same is true for the School of Prophets. It got a subsequent boost about 500 years before Jesus (we'll cover this later). It declined again. However it got a boost roughly thirty years prior to Jesus' birth, when a couple pledged their child to the cause - - if they were blessed with a successful pregnancy. They were blessed, but, to the dismay of many, that child was a girl. They named her Judy. Nonetheless they followed through on their pledge.

The Essenes then rebooted themselves and got to work re-studying and copying ancient Jewish texts. They were especially focused on the fulfillment of those prophecies about "The Coming of the Messiah". Their community was essentially a commune. They were vegetarians. They wore white robes. Communicating with Angels was accepted, as was immortality and pre-existence (past lives). They were very much aware of the Precession of the Equinox and the Age of Pisces associated with the coming of the Messiah.

The Age of Pisces, the Age of Aquarius, etc., are nothing more than the Precession of the Equinox conveniently split up into "months". These months (the names) don't really mean anything. Each of these "months" is about 2000 years long. Now you understand why there is a current "debate" now on whether there should be 12 or 13 signs of the zodiac. That's because currently there are 12, but 13 works better because 13 x 2000 = 26,000 years. You've seen the latter number in our discussions many times.

Thus the Essenes were far more than just another Jewish sect. They were into exactly the things I have talked about throughout this book. They knew these things were real, e.g., immortality, talking with Angels, and pre-existence. They also encouraged astrology, psychic development, and had influences from Persia, India, and Egypt. It was a very diverse group that included Jews and Gentiles alike.

There were males around, for sure, but the women were suddenly quite important. (Interestingly, please note again that "female" is supposed to become the new mode of doing business.) Judy became their leader at Mt. Carmel, and played a major role in educating Jesus (we'll get to this).

11.2 The Wise Men

Zermada was a woman outside the Essene community and yet played a key role as well. A Phoenician from the Roman Province of Syria, she no doubt would have been burned at the stake a few centuries later. Her own psychic abilities told her that a Messiah would be borne in Judea. Thus she traveled to, and took up residence at, Mt. Carmel. She and Judy had a close relationship. She was an astrologer, dream interpreter, and meditator. She taught and helped guide the Essenes. Since Mt. Carmel was not her home, she still traveled, and thus provided a vital link to far away lands - - like places where Wise Men live.

When the Wise Men came, they first visited the Romans, then Judy, then Herod, and finally Bethlehem. Their trip was a counterclockwise trip of well over 500 miles -- one way. There are different suggestions about what the Star of Bethlehem really was. Maybe it was a conjunction (close togetherness) of the planets Saturn and Jupiter, a comet, or even a myth based on the star Sirius and Egypt. Regardless, Zermada provides the missing link regarding the Wise Men.

It turns out that Wise Men also came from Egypt, India, as well as Tibet to greet the newborn -- basically all at the same time.

11.3 *John the Baptist*

John the Baptist became the prophesied forerunner of Jesus. John was Jesus' cousin, and they very much knew one another. All of this was highly coordinated by the Essenes, whose self imposed role was to see that the prophecies were fulfilled. It was very much like a play. Once the Essenes studied the ancient texts, the play script was right there in front of them. They then went out of their way to make sure it happened the way it was forecasted to be. They directed the play and chose the supporting actors.

There was plenty of turmoil in the area when rumors of John and Jesus surfaced. Thus Zermada, Judy, and others resorted to secret meetings and the like. Mary spent much time during her pregnancy with Elizabeth (John's mother) "hiding out in the hills" away from the mainstream public.

11.4 *Mary and Joseph*

[Link 1102] The Essenes played it safe regarding the birth of Jesus. They carefully chose twelve girls, age 4, that represented the twelve tribes of Israel (I agree that this could also mean the twelve signs of the zodiac, i.e., the twelve months of the 26,000 year cycle) and raised them as part of the commune. These were the best of the best spiritually, physically, and mentally. At age 12-13, the day came to choose one to be the Mother of Jesus, and that's when the magic occurred.

At daybreak of that day, as they were climbing the stairs to the altar as part of the daily ritual, thunder and lightening occurred. An Angel appeared (Gabriel) and took Mary's hand and escorted her to the top of the altar. This was the sign the Essenes were looking for. Josie, who was next to Mary during this magical event, pledged her life to caring for Jesus.

The above is from Cayce. Drunvalo, or more precisely Thoth, provides more insight. Akhenaten's 300 immortal Egyptians, who successfully "graduated" from his Mystery School, were nearly all women. They waited until about 500 B.C. (about 800 years from Akhenaten's time) and formed the Essene Brotherhood. These 300 became its inner circle. Mary was one of these immortals.

Jesus was human, just like you and me, but his soul was from the highest level. Through his own hard work, he had learned how to resurrect. Ascension and resurrection lead to the same end, but are very different techniques. Ascension is far more traditional, yet also far more difficult if you are of duality consciousness. Resurrection solves that problem. More on this topic later, but at least you can begin to understand why Jesus came, i.e., there are technical issues with duality consciousness.

The Essenes chose Joseph to be the husband. Joseph, per Cayce, was not happy when he learned of the pregnancy. He was 36 and she was 16 at the time. He eventually came around, of course. Ten years after the birth of Jesus, he and Mary had their own children.

11.5 The Trip to Bethlehem

[Link 1104] The trip to Bethlehem was a big deal for the Essenes to orchestrate. They accompanied Mary and Joseph en route as well as kept watch in Bethlehem. Mary was very pregnant, having to make the week long journey to register for taxation. Elizabeth and others had to go as well. There was indeed "no room at the inn" because so many were there to register. The innkeeper was also an Essene, and his daughter played a major role with other Essenes in ultimately locating the stable under a hill. This out of the way location also kept the crowds away, who ridiculed the couple's age difference and provided general privacy.

11.6 Herod

[Link 1105] Herod is famous for his massacre of the infants. What prompted this horrendous massacre? Cayce provides the inside scoop. Judy, the leader of the Essenes at this time, had kept in contact with the various Wise Men of far-away lands. Protocol was followed, and thus the Romans were notified of the visitors and their intentions. Readings were given for the Roman soldier who actually guided them to Bethlehem. Visiting Herod was not protocol, and should not have been included in the visit. Judy proposed the visit because she hoped that Herod would become enraged, and thus cause turmoil between him and the Roman rulers. Herod had been a ruthless tyrant for 40 years, and she and the Jewish leaders wanted him out.

Herod indeed became enraged when the Wise Men returned home - - without telling him where the infant was located. The Romans tried, unsuccessfully, to stop the subsequent murders. Cayce provides readings on several women who lost their infants, including one for Eunice - - a friend of Elizabeth. He also provides insight on Herod's wife who took interest in the Essenes and actually saved some of the children. Herod died of cancer a few years later and, typical of his behavior, had his wife murdered just prior.

11.6 Essenes' Link to Egypt

As you likely know, Jesus' family fled to Egypt during this horrific time. They could have gone anywhere to hide from Herod. They chose Egypt, in part, because they wanted to fulfill the prophecies.

In addition, the Essenes had the strong historical link to Egypt via the Tat Brotherhood, which are the 300 immortals mentioned above. Both Cayce and Thoth (through Drunvalo) confer on this point. Cayce refers to it simply as the Brotherhood. Tat was the son of Thoth and was assigned its leader. Thus it's been called the Brotherhood, the Tat Brotherhood, and the Essene Brotherhood.

Being immortal, these 300 individuals can be born unto Earth at any time in the future. Thus some were conveniently born (again) just in time for Jesus. They remember everything from their past lives. This comes in real handy if you have a job to do when you show back up on Earth! (We discuss immortality below.)

I don't know the "mission statement" of the Tat Brotherhood, yet a really good guess is to "get us back where we belong", i.e., ultimately to get us on the new grid, thus undoing the Great Fall.

The immortal Essenes formed the crucial inner circle of the Essene community during the time of Jesus. Per Thoth, and as mentioned above, Mary was one of these. I don't know if John the Baptist was or was not. I would not be surprised.

Incidentally, Jesus was not part of the Tat Brotherhood. He is far more advanced. Jesus was instead part of the Order of Melchizedek, which is a much higher Order, and also a very misunderstood topic. We'll cover this in a later chapter.

This chronological story resumes in the next chapter, which focuses on Jesus. Meanwhile, the remaining sections here provide important details of immortality and the resurrection processes. Jesus is very much a part of this conversation as well.

11.7 Immortality

Exactly what is immortality? What is everlasting life? The Bible talks about Noah and others as being 600 years old or more. If he was in the same human body all that time, then the modern medical community had better study him! Is this everlasting life?

How about Mary? Assuming she "showed up" 500 years earlier in the Essene community, how was it that she was only 16 when she became pregnant with Jesus? Per Thoth's own writings [4], he's 50,000 years old or more and showed up as Arlich, Thoth, Hermes, and maybe others. Jesus grew and aged as well, and upon resurrection came back just as aged as he was prior to the crucifixion.

So what's the deal? Exactly what are these people? They "returned" as being younger, older, and even the same appearance as before. What is at the core of their existence? What defines their existence? What defines your existence? When you die, what goes with you? What goes to Heaven?

The Terminator (in the movie) showed up with a computer in his body. What do we show up with?

The primary tool for immortality is a well-tuned chakra system. For simplicity, simply imagine the 7.23 cm energy of the universe. It contacts your chakra system, which directs it to your DNA, and your DNA magically manifests your physical body in one big "poof". Your neighbor has slightly different DNA, so his/her body is slightly different.

Here on Earth, our bodies naturally deteriorate. Thus we need to feed ourselves, exercise, etc. Everywhere else (4th level and beyond) we don't age. We don't need food. We don't need anything physically. Our bodies don't deteriorate. They simply remain as the corresponding DNA dictates.

If you are immortal and come "down" to Earth, you have a couple of ways of getting here, and a couple of ways of leaving. The "getting here" and "leaving here" is the hard part, and that's what the Mystery School and the Great Pyramid "graduation" was all about. If you conquer these transitions, then you are inherently immortal. Immortality is simply the by-product of learning how to transition between the different levels. Thus, in and of itself, immortality is no big deal.

There are two ways to conquer this transition. One is ascension. That's literally "beam me up Scotty" in Star Trek. You are sitting in your chair one moment, and then, in the blink of an eye, you are gone. Your physical body goes with you, along with your chakra system. You show up on the other side. Your well-tuned chakra system is what actually carried your body through the transition.

Jesus, as stated earlier, "invented" the resurrection system. In this case your physical body actually dies on this side, and you re-create it once you reach the other side. It's a subtle, but very important, difference from ascension.

Jesus created resurrection [1] because of the Great Fall, and especially because we are of duality consciousness. The normal mode of operation in the heavens is ascension. The Atlanteans (the Adam and Eve race) were nicely en route to learning ascension, but the Great Fall occurred and all that progress was destroyed.

We certainly could have started over, but that would have taken several hundred thousand years [1] for the masses to learn ascension from scratch (poor Mother Earth!). But it's obvious that God agreed that's not the best plan, and instead agreed with this synthetic 13,000 year fast-track plan based on the Grid.

Thus the masses, in general, are not going to be experts in ascension with only 13,000 years of training. That's why Jesus came.

Keep on reading to learn the details.

11.8 *Memory & Resurrection*

Our Sacred Geometry discussions gave us "form". It gave us our bodies. The piano notes gave us the heavens. The sine wave gives us "time".

The chakra system provides immortality, i.e., continuity between different bodies and the different heavens. (Incidentally the chakra system itself is of Sacred Geometry structure.)

But there is still something missing.

Pretend I just died, yet I am communicating with you in your sleep or whatever. I'm probably in a different body or have no body. I may be in a different heaven. Time may even be different for me, yet I am communicating with you.

What's the deal? How do I know you? My Earthly memory is gone. How do I even know myself? Go ahead and scratch your head on this one.

Everything has to be simple, and this is indeed a simple question.

The answer lies in what's called the Akashic Records or God's Book of Remembrance.

All of our intentions, actions, and essentially everything is recorded in a place that you and I simply can't conceive of. The analogy would be on a storage device, like a thumb drive or hard drive, in another dimension where there's no such thing as actual physical objects.

This location is what the Bible refers to as the Book of Life and/or the Book of Remembrance when it implies we'll each be judged at the Gates of Heaven. You can put on a three-piece suit and a big smile at the Gates, but the reality is that there is indeed a record.

Recall that some indigenous tribes had to "repent their sins" before the grid could be fully functional. The Book of Life never forgets.

If you are immortal and flying around from this dimension to that dimension, these records are you. Immortals indeed have full memory of their past, including all their past lives in other heavens. That's because their well-tuned chakra system inherently gives them access to these records. These are known outside the Christian world as the Akashic Records, and they are very real.

Edgar Cayce was able to access the Akashic Records of others [Link 1101], and he was astonishingly accurate. This is why they are called "readings". He was actually reading their Akashic Records (Then the poor guy had to translate them somehow into English so those listening could actually "hear".)

Notice how simple this is. The truth is always simple.

Incidentally, Cayce remembered nothing when he woke up. He was always exhausted afterward.

11.9 Jesus' Main Purpose

He had to go through death and the corresponding resurrection process (re-creating his body on the other side). By doing this, the actual resurrection "recipe" got stored in the Akashic Records. This is the reason Jesus came. He came here to die. In the meantime he did lots of other stuff, but his primary reason was to go through this resurrection process, setting the precedent. Per Thoth [1], this was planned long in advance of his arrival here on Earth.

11.10 Reincarnation

The title of this section is really "Reincarnation: Blame the Bad Guys".

We've covered immortality just above, and now you know how spiritual entities remember who they are as they move around.

However, what about the rest of us here on Earth? How did the Great Fall affect our immortality potential and our own Akashic Records? First, your Akashic Records are still there, and you are still very much being "recorded".

Regarding immortality, the Great Fall ruined our potential to ascend -- delaying it by many 100,000 years of learning. Now we are cramming all that into this 13,000 year fast-track program.

Thus we (that's you and me) are very much in limbo. Akhenaten managed to create the 300 immortals, yet that took a university and several years of intense hands-on training. Since then, perhaps a few others somehow made it, but whatever that number is, it's a micro-fraction of the 7 billion people on this planet. It's these latter masses that this conversation is about.

This is also where "reincarnation" makes its entry into our conversation. Past lives is one thing (immortals do that as well), but reincarnation is completely different. It is the direct result of the Great Fall.

Reincarnation results from you physically dying here on Earth - - and that's it. You indeed go to the other side, up to a point. However, since you did not ascend (bring your body with you) or resurrect (re-create it upon arrival), then you can only spend a brief time there. It's not possible for you to exist long-term on the other side without bringing your body. Thus you go back and try again, and hope the next time you indeed bring your body via one of these two techniques. This recycling is what reincarnation is.

Jesus did us a great favor and "stored" the resurrection process (e.g., the instructions) in the Akashic Records. Just like Edgar Cayce accessed the records of others, we can now access these records of Jesus.

Has anyone (such as your friends and relatives) actually accessed those records and thus resurrected since Jesus' time? I'm certainly in no position to make that call. My guess is yes - - I imagine a few "advanced souls" have indeed done so.

However, the masses definitely have not. That's because the 4th level grid repair was not yet complete. Was there even any place to go to? Per Drunvalo, each of us has gone around 1,000 times each. We are immortal beings whose efforts to ascend repeatedly fail.

Edgar Cayce, in addition to the medical readings, also did past life readings (and much more). It's fascinating to realize that numerous individuals, who were right there asking Edgar Cayce questions, were around in Jesus' time.

.

He talked with individuals who had previously been Judy, Zermada, Herod's wife, Jesus' sister Ruth and his brother Jude, Elizabeth (the mother of John the Baptist), Eunice (a friend of John the Baptist's mother), the roman soldier who married Ruth, and more. These individuals came to Cayce by their own free will. To me that's fascinating in and of itself. Then one day Cayce got the urge to move to Ohio, and there came another surge of "Jesus" folks.

Reincarnation is a very sensitive subject for some. It is not important that you accept it. It's your intentions and actions that count.

Again, it's time for the plane to take off, yet we first have to leave all that ego-luggage behind. We must get aligned in our intentions, thus accepting the differences between you and me, and then fasten our seat belts and trust the airplane to the captain.

Chapter 12

- Jesus -

Jesus was obviously a great person. However, he definitely had his Earthly entourage well before, during, and after his birth. This was the Essenes and then his disciples and friends. If this was a rock concert, the disciples would be on stage with him, and the Essenes would take care of everything else - - including the tour bus and preparations.

- - - - Edgar Cayce 254:109 - - - -

"Hence the group we refer to here as the Essenes, which was the outgrowth of the periods of preparation from the Melchizedek, as propagated by Elijah and Llisha and Samuel ...."

- - - - - - - -

The Essenes thus took charge, and this means getting up each morning and looking at their hit list to see that both Jesus and the prophecies were well taken care of. We've already covered, per Cayce, how Mary was chosen from the twelve chosen maidens. The Essene community assigned Joseph as the husband. Just prior to the wedding ceremony, an Angel appeared and told Mary she was pregnant with the very special child of "immaculate" conception.

Meanwhile John, the cousin of Jesus and son of Elizabeth, was likewise supported by the Essenes as being the prophesized forerunner to Jesus. John was six months older than Jesus.

We already covered the birth of Jesus, Herod's massacre, and now we continue.

12.1 The Trip to Egypt

Let's get back to the family's trip to Egypt [Link 1201]. The Essenes protected Jesus en route. This was serious business for them. Essene parties were scouting things out well ahead of, and likewise providing protection behind, the traveling family. Josie, who had pledged to care for Jesus, went as well.

A primary goal was to spend time in Alexandria, where prior Essene records were kept. Josie was instructed to study such in the Alexandria library and to relate her findings back to Mt. Carmel. This included astrological studies, prophecies, etc.

On the return trip from Egypt, food was sparse, yet the amount of food would mysteriously increase. Thus Jesus was performing such psychic miracles even as an infant. Also, both he and his clothes had a healing affect on those who came into contact.

12.2 The Education of Jesus

[Link 1202, Link 1203] When they returned from Egypt, they ended up at Mt. Carmel. This was so Jesus could be trained by the Essenes, and in particular Judy. She educated him in Mosaic Law - - until he was about twelve - - and also about the teachings of the prophets.

This is crucial training for Jesus. When he would subsequently meet and have conflicts with Jewish leaders, this schooling provided his foundation. These leaders were amazed at how this twelve-year old kid could hold his own, and much more, in such debates.

Jesus then traveled to Syria, Persia, and India. So begins the "missing years". Again he was supported by the extensive Essene network in these areas. He was being taught about, and how to master, his spiritual body. Some of these teachers were the actual Wise Men who came to Bethlehem at his birth.

Although he was very gifted at birth (an understatement) and was immortal, he was still new at being in a human body. Thus he had to learn how to manage that body - - spiritually. He also had to learn to deal with duality consciousness (thanks to Lucifer) and not let his ego get in the way. These are probably the types of topics he studied. This work simultaneously fine-tuned his psychic abilities, which inherently include his famous halo. Your success in ascending or resurrecting is very much linked to all of these issues. Furthermore, these abilities, in you and me at least, are prevalent early in life - - yet can decrease significantly around puberty. Thus Jesus may have needed a "booster shot" in this regard.

After returning from Persia for his father's funeral, he then went to Egypt, where he spent the greatest amount of his missing years. He further studied the library materials at Alexandria. (Thanks to Alexander the Great, Alexandria was the world's library. Sadly much of those library materials were destroyed by an attack around 270 AD.)

12.3 Final Preps for the Ministry

[Link 1203] John went to Egypt months earlier than Jesus. Once Jesus left Alexandria, he joined John at the pyramids. Both went to the Mystery School. Cayce says they were in different classes. Just as in Akhenaten's day, the final graduation was in the Great Pyramid itself. Here they both faced death, exactly like Akhenaten's immortals had to do, by leaving their bodies. They ascended momentarily, and then came back. This is what the Great Pyramid is for - - practice - - so that, when you actually die, your fears don't get in the way.

Upon their success in the Great Pyramid, Jesus was now ready to return and begin his formal ministry. To fulfill the prophecies, John went ahead of him and laid the public foundation for that ministry. Imagine that you are John, and you just graduated from this amazing real-life experience. I'm sure he was quite excited - - much like "born again" people get excited - - only multiply that a hundred-fold.

Upon returning to Judea, John assumed the role of marketing manager. This was to fulfill the prophecies, and the Essenes made sure that such was indeed done.

- - - - Matthew 3:3 - - - -

For this is he that was spoken of by the Prophet Esaias, saying The voice of one crying in the wilderness, Prepare ye the way of the Lord, make his paths straight ..

- - - - - - - -

Marketing-wise, John had a very good niche product - - Jesus! There was no internet in those days, no TV, no printing. Thus marketing was limited to essentially the town crier and word of mouth. Thus John made himself appear as an outcast and became the "town crier" in the wilderness.

Baptism was an Essene custom, representing purification. However, John went a step further and, when Jesus finally arrived in the Jordan

River for his initiation, John fully submerged him. Per Cayce, this represented their Great Pyramid experience all over again, as it ceremoniously is death (submerging) followed by life again. Thus, depending on your religious inclinations, this represents immortality, ascension, resurrection, going to Heaven, etc.

At this point Jesus himself took another deep breath of preparation, and went into the wilderness for his final initiation.

- - - - Luke 4:1-2 - - - -

And Jesus being full of the Holy Ghost returned from Jordan, and was led by the Spirit into the wilderness, being forty days tempted of the devil. And in those days he did eat nothing: and when they were ended, he afterward hungered ....

- - - - - - - - -

Cayce explained what Jesus accomplished there. It relates to the duality consciousness problem. However, it clarifies that Jesus had a past (before Mary brought him into our world) where he had confronted the Lucifer issue, and had done some selfish things. Thus in my opinion, and just like the rest of us, Jesus had his own sins that he had to confront. Not only that, to achieve his purpose (to resurrect) he had to be of perfect unity consciousness, unaffected by the pulls of Lucifer's duality consciousness, free will, and his ego.

He therefore had to repent then and there in the wilderness, and do whatever else was required to emerge of pure unity consciousness - - and remain so until his death. (Apparently he did just that - - judging by all the miracles!)

Thus Jesus began his ministry.

12.4 The Ministry

[Link 1204, Link 1205] Cayce gave a reading for Andrew, a disciple of both John and then Jesus. Andrew encouraged his older brother Peter to also become a disciple. Although it's commonly thought that the disciples were poor, this is not the case. The disciples John and James, as well as Matthew, were of wealthy families and had good connections. Most of the disciples were from the northern end of the Jordon River (Sea of Galilee). Judas was from the southern end of the Jordon River (the Dead Sea), and thus had different views from the others.

Jesus indeed changed the water into wine during a wedding. The wine was running unexpectedly short, and that was simply unacceptable. Mary, Jesus' mother, was responsible for the food and the feast of the wedding. Mary recalled then that Jesus had increased the food, as an infant, during their return trip from Egypt. She thus connected the dots and asked him to do it again. In many ways this was a test because his mom wanted to know if he had been successful in the wilderness. (Also recall that it's easier to do these things as a child than as an adult following puberty.) Further recall that Mary was immortal (per Thoth) and was of the inner circle of the Essenes. Thus she knew exactly what she was asking, and why. Jesus responded like a rebellious teenager might, somewhat complaining to his mom that such tricks for the sake an everyday party is not what his calling is.

- - - - John 2:4 - - - -

Jesus saith unto her, Woman, what have I to do with thee? Mine hour is not yet come ....

· · · · · · · · ·

Nonetheless, he willfully obliged, and the rest is history.

━━━━━━━━━━

Jesus indeed changed the water to wine, multiplied the loaves of bread, and as an infant maintained the food supply for the trip home from Egypt. This is easily done on the higher levels. It's modus operandi. However, it's far more difficult on the 3rd level, but such is indeed being done by children these days. Here is a link for a few such examples [Link 1206].

My favorite example is a six-year old girl who gave the audience a thousand unopened rosebuds, and she proceeded to have them all open at the same moment upon the wave of her hand. Many kids being borne now have advanced souls - - not nearly as advanced as Jesus, but nonetheless more advanced than the rest of us. They have a lot to teach us during these critical times. This link explains more about the children being born now, and also talks about the related ADD issue [Link 1207].

These miracles are fundamentally powered by Love (unity consciousness) and a well-tuned chakra system. The halo of Jesus is another result of that chakra system. Notice that his halo is always has four, or more, "rods" supporting it. The "center" of those rods is the pineal gland which is in the exact middle of your head. When you reach puberty, the pineal gland can get encrusted in deposits (like arthritis).

Thus you need to actually use that gland so it does not shrink and/or get encrusted, or you will lose these abilities. Indigenous tribes address this problem with their youth. That pineal gland is your third eye (See chakra figure further below). It's your unity consciousness eye.

12.5 Jesus also Healed

The mechanism is different for healing as opposed to creating the above miracles. It's a bit easier to do because the healing force comes more from the center of your body (the navel area) instead the heart.

Although there is healing of the hands (reiki), chanting, and other methods used to heal, I'm convinced that it's just Love. Love is the healer, and all these different means exist because the person doing the healing believes that particular method works best for them. It's much like a placebo effect for the healer.

Regardless, you are truly loving the person when healing occurs. Perhaps this is why and how Jesus unknowingly healed as an infant. His body and clothes were simply full of that real unconditional Love for all, which is unity consciousness. You treat everyone as if you are one.

This is why the Bible is full of the healings of Jesus. They are relatively easy.

12.6 Ye Must Be Born Again

Nicodemus was one of the few, if not the only, Jewish leader (Pharisee) who accepted the teachings of Jesus. Jesus taught him as they met secretly at night. He informed Nicodemus that the Jewish traditions are fine, yet to see the kingdom of God, Jesus said the following:

- - - - John 3:3 - - - -

Jesus answered and said unto him Verily, verily, I say unto thee, Except a man be born again, he cannot see the kingdom of God"

- - - - - - - -

To help interpret this Cayce says:

- - - - Edgar Cayce 262: 60 - - - -

"Ye must be born ... of the spirit and through the flesh ...."

- - - - - - - -

Cayce proceeded to use the example of Moses raising his rod, which in turn parts the sea, which then frees the people of Israel from their bondage in Egypt. For me, this is a fascinating analogy.

To better understand, let's look at the technology, which is the chakras in your body.

Just like the 7 primary piano notes, you have 7 primary chakras in your body. Being born again is associated with the first time that you actually experience your Heart chakra. So yes.... we finally have to look at your chakra system. Incidentally, this "system" is what Jesus used to create his healings and miracles. It is also a remarkable Sacred Geometry system at work.

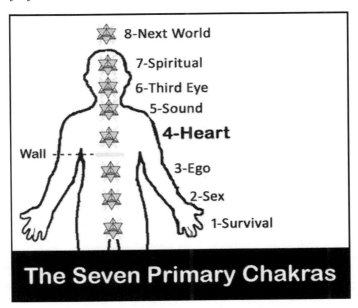

When you are a newborn, you cling to chakra #1, which is basic survival. (This is where your original 8 cells are located.) You are in this strange new place and need something to hang onto. Once you are comfortable with that, you begin to explore chakra #2. That's essentially your mother's breast, since it's literally staring you in the face, but it's really about making physical contact with the world around you. Think of this as the first time your spirit has actually "touched" anything. Imagine that! I always imagine babies squeezing your finger in their tiny little hand. They are exploring.

Then, once you get comfortable with touching objects, you start exploring more non-physical contact. This, for example, results in the terrible twos - - when you want to know how everything works and what your limits are.

Chakra #3 is the ego - - or certainly prompts the ego. This is what Jesus had to contend with during his 40 days. Inside his body is this ego-trap, and he has to not be consumed or tormented by it as he travels, preaches, creates miracles, heals, and ultimately dies. He is not used to having this "thing" (chakra #3) in his body if he came from above.

For lots of people on Earth, and especially the materialistic individuals and criminals, their world consists of only these three chakras. Collectively these represent basic survival in the world. They are readily available to everyone - - as the consolation prize of simply being born.

Now notice the wall (symbolically) shown between the 3rd and 4th chakras. That was put there by God, so we don't "abuse" the system. That 4th chakra is the Heart chakra, and the first one associated with unity consciousness. When you (somehow) manage to get there the first time, you get this incredible rush of awareness. Suddenly you realize that there's a lot more to your world than you ever imagined. You are suddenly just overwhelmed with bliss, potential, and many other emotions.

That's the feeling of being "born again". You are born again of the spirit, but you are still in the flesh. You get your first real glimpse of unity consciousness (or oneness with God, or going to Heaven, etc.) and its power.

This is most likely what Jesus meant. He was telling Nicodemus that unity consciousness (4th chakra and above) is the pathway to oneness with God, i.e., to the kingdom of God. Going through your daily routines, including religious routines, isn't going to do it. You need to somehow get out of your box and truly experience those higher chakras. In the Great Pyramid, Jesus and John went all the way. By successfully accomplishing this, your soul is (more) connected to God, yet you are still in your earthly body.

People get that "rush of excitement" in various situations. I've seen it during Christian concerts with youths. For me it happened when I first read Cayce's biography, and learned of the Angel actually visiting him. For others it happened on LSD or some other psychedelic drug.

Indigenous tribes sometimes employ this method via their blend of ceremonial plants. For others it was through a near death experience. Some of these experiences go beyond the 4th chakra to higher chakras. As stated above Jesus and John went "all the way" in the Great Pyramid.

Again, I find it fascinating that Cayce used the example of Moses raising his rod to part the sea. "Raising the rod" is symbolically getting past that wall between the 3rd and 4th chakras.

Nonetheless, being born again implies that you go beyond using just your first three chakras. This enables your spirit to be born, or simply woken up, following the birth of your actual physical body.

———————

Jesus also advised Nicodemus:

- - - - John 3:13 - - - -

"And no man hath ascended up to heaven, but he that came down from heaven, even the Son of man which is in heaven .."

⸺ ⸺ ⸺ ⸺ ⸺ ⸺ ⸺

Per Cayce, this implies that not only did Jesus come from "above", all of us did - - and all of us are going back assuming we use the tools that are within us.

12.7 Raising of the Dead

[Link 1208] Jesus performed several truly miraculous raisings of the dead. I am equally in awe. Per Jesus, the healing of the blind man and Lazarus' illness and death were "for the glory of God". What does this mean?

Everyone has their answer to this question. My interpretation is based on the big picture. The Great Pyramid was built. The Egyptian and Sumerian cultures blossomed with respect for unity consciousness. Then Akhenaten's 300 immortals were born. They then returned to become the Essenes, to raise Jesus, and to assure the prophecies were fulfilled. Meanwhile the 83,000 structures of the grid were built, or being built, around the world. The Precession of the Equinox time clock is ticking away, and getting close.

With seemingly perfect timing, Jesus shows up right in the midst of the most religiously controversial area of the world. He initiated himself in the Great Pyramid to complete his schooling. He did a few miracles and healings here and there to get attention.

Then, as his final act, he raised the dead - - fully knowing that the world would sit upright in their chairs. Jesus fully knows that with this attention comes his death.

The Essenes have pretty much done their part, and at this point are simply watching.

Jesus now does the final act of the play.

He chose to come. He came to store the resurrection recipe in the Akashic Records, so that all of us trapped souls can get out of this mess created by Murphy's Law, i.e., the Lucifer Experiment (duality consciousness) combined with the Great Fall (the bad-guys).

He knows he's going to die. He needs to. He plans to. Notice how his miracles got "bigger and bigger" as he progressed through his ministry. He could have just as easily healed Lazarus, or someone else, on day #1. That's not a good marketing campaign. Everyone will expect that to happen every day thereafter. The campaign might have just fizzled.

Instead he went about it correctly. He started slow, and not too visibly, and generated followers and much respect. He got his following together, which is the disciples, his friends and families, and their friends and families. He did lots of healings, etc., for these folks and thus created a very solid following upon his departure. He generated followers even in the hard core Jewish leader population, and helped them deal with the apparent religious conflicts. Through it all, he was trying to explain what it's all about. That was, and still is, the toughest job of all because we are all asleep.

Finally, he started raising the dead. That's a good way to wake people up - - even if just for a few minutes. It is also a way to upset the rulers, whose goal is just that - - to rule others, i.e., power driven egos. That's exactly what Jesus did. He intentionally delayed showing his "power" (raising the dead) until it was time to orchestrate his own death. The time had come for the final act.

12.8 The Final Act

[Link 1208] Per Cayce, Jesus' donkey ride into Jerusalem on Good Friday was set up in advance with the woman who owned the donkey.

The two disciples, who Jesus sent to get it, were unaware of the plan and amazingly found this donkey tied up exactly where Jesus said it would be.

Cayce also provides details on the Last Supper, such as the actual menu, the physical attributes of Jesus (including his weight, eye color, hair color, fingernails, etc.) and likewise the disciples. The robe Jesus wore had been woven by Martha, the wife of Nicodemus. She got the idea when she first learned that John and Jesus were in Egypt, achieving their initiations. It was a single piece, very light gray.

Likewise, Cayce provides the mood. Jesus was joking even during the betrayal moments. He was completely aware of what was taking place. The recently discovered Book of Judas says that Jesus and Judas conferred on the betrayal. During the trial and sentencing, Jesus thrived in the satisfaction that he was finally fulfilling what he'd set out to do.

12.9 The Resurrection

[Link 1209] Per Cayce, upon his death, Jesus' burial clothing fell to the ground. This is significant. Thus his physical Earthly body had indeed "disintegrated" or, more accurately, simply disappeared and became nothing. He then resurrected, and that (by definition) required him to re-create his physical body. That takes time. When he subsequently asked Mary Magdalene not to touch him in the garden, Cayce clarifies that she would have been electrically shocked. That's because the resurrection process was not yet complete.

This electrical behavior is very well understood, and it very much relates the electrical (and magnetic) fields associated with your chakra system. Once Jesus became more so "solid", he himself was electrically grounded and therefore safe for Mary to touch.

At this point Jesus' mission was complete. He made himself visible to a few, to make sure that the news of his resurrection got out, but he did not start another ministry, etc. He quickly disappeared from the limelight. I presume his marketing manager told him to "quit while you are ahead"!

If you look around today, 2000 years later, it's mind boggling how many churches there are (and disappointing as to how many different churches there are). There is little doubt in my mind that his "marketing manager" planned on this 2000 year window to get the word out. What I mean by this is Jesus did not come on Dec 21, 2012. He came much earlier so we'd be ready by about that timeframe.

Every major religion in the world has Jesus and/or his teachings in it. Religion is a tool to help people cope with the "why we are here" question. Many people are capable of coping on their own, without needing a church or reading the Bible, and still - - Jesus and/or his teaching are typically right there in the palms of their hands as well.

If we go back to the airplane analogy, Jesus essentially brought this massive airplane to the gate. By going through the resurrection process, and storing that in the Akashic Records, he made it possible for the non-perfect masses to get on board.

This remarkable marketing campaign by the Essenes, then Jesus himself, and finally by the efforts of the church, scripture writers, and word of mouth have definitely gotten the word out. Job well done!

Chapter 13

- Who was Jesus -

There is a fascinating character in the Bible. His name is Melchizedek, and there's very little information about him. Nonetheless Link 1601 does an excellent job of tying together these few Biblical passages. Here's the gist.

He lived about the time of Abraham, arguably around 2,000 B.C. He was a very high priest of seemingly wizard quality.

- - - - Genesis 14:18 - - - -

And Melchizedek King of Salem brought forth bread and wine; and he was the priest of the most high God

- - - - - - - -

- - - - Genesis Hebrews 7:1, 2 - - - -

For this Melchizedek, king of Salem, priest of the most high God, who met Abraham returning from the slaughter of the kings, and blessed him; To whom also Abraham gave a tenth part of all; first being by interpretation King of righteousness, and after that also King of Salem, which is, King of Peace ...

- - - - - - - -

Aaron was the older brother of Moses, his spokesperson, and thus the first high priest mentioned in the Bible. The history of Moses and its Aaronic Priesthood had been around for 16 centuries (since roughly the time of Akhenaten) when Jesus appeared as the new kid on the block.

Understandably there was confusion and resentment, especially in view of the following.

- - - - Hebrews 6:20 - - - -

Whither the forerunner is for us entered, even Jesus, made a high priest forever after the Order of Melchizedek ...

13.1 The Order of Melchizedek

Thus, per the above, we now have the Aaronic priesthood, Melchizedek, and Jesus. Who's the head honcho here? Then there's the Order of Melchizedek. What's that all about? What's an order?

If that's not enough to ponder, the subject of "Who was Jesus" is very much a debated topic. For Christians, Jesus is the son of God. For Muslims, he is a prophet to Mohammed. For some Jewish populations, Jesus is a prophet preparing the world for God's apocalyptic overthrow of the evil forces. Buddha represented everything that Jesus represented – essentially unity consciousness. The list goes on and on.

I am going to add yet another chair to this table of debate. However, I'm not going to do so by arguing scriptures. We've been doing that for 2,000 years, and we are still doing it.

We have to look elsewhere for the answer. Throughout this book, I've intentionally kept the math as the negotiating tool that allows me, with good confidence, to argue my points. In addition to that, there is an incredible amount of new information pouring in. This is the information age. A hundred years ago we were on horseback, including the President. Now we can pick up a phone and have instant access to an astronaut on Mars. We have individuals who can travel to Mars instantly in their mind and give us detailed information, including the serial numbers off the equipment. (This is "remote viewing" and was part of the U.S. government's Stargate program)

A mind-blowing amount of information is available on the web, including information on ancient texts, new archaeological discoveries, new spiritual technologies, string theory, what the bad-guys are up to, opinions on everything, and on and on. Edgar Cayce showed up. Thoth showed up (again) through Drunvalo. Channeling and other esoteric phenomena are everywhere. This surge of information and technology is no accident. It's helping us get aboard the airplane. It's helping us answer questions - - exactly like the Jesus question here.

Thus, using all this new information and associated forensics, here's my view of who is Jesus.

Per Drunvalo1, there are 72 orders in our universe. These are like offices in a corporation. The Order of Melchizedek, of which Drunvalo is a part of, is what I refer to as the QA department (Quality Assurance). It is the highest, or one of the highest, orders in our universe.

These are individuals who have successfully reached the highest level in our universe (the highest note in the piano's octave). Where do you go to from there? You are definitely "One with God" at that point. Per Drunvalo, you either choose to stay in, or leave, our universe. If you leave, you go to the next universe (the next octave on the piano). If you choose to stay, then you essentially do another cycle around our universe, and your job is to fix problems. You share your wisdom, and become even wiser as a result.

That is what the Order of Melchizedek does. It fixes problems. It is exactly like the Quality Assurance Department in a corporation. The remaining 71 orders are simply other job positions in the corporation. For example, one is the Tat Brotherhood. These were the 300 Akhenaten immortals, many of which created the Essenes about 500 B.C. It seems they also highly influenced Greece at the same time, and England (we cover this later). Whatever else they have done, or are currently doing, is unknown - - at least to me - - but I imagine they are quite busy, even today.

Another order, called the Brotherhood of the Seven Rays [1], will help out with the "airplane". Those of you who successfully ascend or resurrect will do just that. You get the first class seats. The rest of us are crammed into the coach section of the airplane, and will be cared for by this order. Humorously, we'll will herded like cattle through the "tunnel", that everyone talks about who's had near death experiences, and make sure that we get through OK.

Whereas the Brotherhood of the Seven Rays and the Tat Brotherhood are dedicated to earthly duties, the Order of Melchizedek's job is to look after the universe as whole. It looks after all the heavens, not just Earth. Thus it's really in the corporate headquarters, whereas these others are the "local divisions".

As the above scriptures state, Jesus is part of the Order of Melchizedek. Unless he's gone on to another universe, he is still around in ours, and a good question is: is he still helping us here on Earth? He's immortal, so he could have easily been here before. Thus he very well could have been the earlier Melchizedek mentioned in Genesis. He could be walking around today and going to Wal-Mart, for all I know. He could likewise be in Heaven and chatting with your relatives there.

In the Biblical arena, this is what the book of HEbrew was trying to say. Jesus is of a higher order than the Aaronic Priesthood, which is Earthly based. The Order of Melchizedek is likewise higher than any Catholic or other earthly-based priesthoods. When you work for the Order of Melchizedek, your domain is the entire universe.

The term "higher" implies exactly what it implies in a corporation. Those individuals are simply far more evolved on the piano notes, and likewise, in unity consciousness. These are very experienced individuals. The universe is simply tapping that experience to make itself better and better, exactly like a corporation does.

Individuality has merit, even on this level.

This should be no surprise as Lucifer, Michael, and Gabriel are indeed unique Angels, i.e., unique individuals. They are not robots. They are not clones. They are individuals. Where did they get their experience?

13.2 *Where did Jesus get His Experience?*

That brings up back to Jesus. Where did Jesus get his experience? It certainly was not by being a carpenter in his back yard. He was also not a programmed robot (Terminator) beamed here to do his stuff.

Even on these highest of levels, you can lead a horse to water but cannot make it drink. The latter is not allowed. Thus Jesus was allowed to come, but he had to tap his own experience, abilities, and motivation to make things happen here on Earth. That is what new presidents of corporations have to do, and that is what Jesus had to do. I'm sure some of you are screaming and yelling at me as you read this, but these insights only put me that much more in awe of Jesus. Think about it. He really did create those miracles and brought the dead back to life. Can you do that? Do you know anyone else who can? Jesus did those things on his own. It truly is amazing. I'd have him on my team anytime!

By contrast, Drunvalo is also of the Order of Melchizedek. (I have no doubt there are others here as well.) He is no Jesus, and in no way has he ever attempted any such comparison. He's just like you and me. His skills, like mine, are analytical. That's why I refer to his work so often. He spent decades learning from nearly every spiritual teacher in the world, studying and practicing all religions, and experiencing all the indigenous tribes worldwide. The point is he had to learn all of this, and decipher it, on his own. He had to learn to meditate, just like you and me, by becoming familiar with his human body. The most powerful spiritual teachers for him were the Native Americans.

All of this took decades of hard work and commitment. He might be a Melchizedek, but he's a long way from being any Jesus.

And just like Jesus, he was not given any special powers, other than those that he brought with him from his prior experience. The only noticeable difference (between Drunvalo and you or me) is he's able to mediate far more clearly and deeply. This allows him to get more ceremonial-type results, and this is precisely why the Mayans invited him into their fold. Drunvalo admits that he never gave ceremony any credence before the Native Americans taught him.

He's always provided classes on how to meditate in preparation for 2012. He had to protect his teaching area because the energy coming off his students (visible to the Military) was repeatedly attracting Black Hawk helicopters - - which interrupted the classes. So, via meditation, he put a force field around it for each conference. The helicopters never bothered the class again, but the military was very interested in how he did it. They insisted he teach them. He did. However, it only works out of Love, so he was more than happy to give the class. You can now better understand why the Mayans knew they had the right man for the job. That's why they chose Drunvalo & Co. to represent the modern population during the Mother Earth ceremonies. The other individuals, who accompanied Drunvalo, had advanced skills as well.

These same skills are what enabled Thoth to communicate with Drunvalo. It's my opinion that Thoth realized there was a communication opportunity, i.e., sufficient skills on the other end of the telephone line. He probably also realized that Drunvalo was an analytical personality, and thus Sacred Geometry could once again be taught to the world. Drunvalo got so excited about Sacred Geometry that he put in many years of hard work. The result is the world is now creating free energy devices based on it. It's my opinion that this is the Order of Melchizedek at work. It employed the experience of Thoth and, in this case, the experience and skills of Drunvalo.

It's relatively recently that Drunvalo received permission to teach how us to connect (to everything everywhere) by going into the heart [3]. This is the ultimate tool for getting through the 2012 transition (humorously, this upgrades your airline ticket so you are no longer in coach). Being there is like being one with God. It's from there that miracles happen. No one has yet turned water to wine, probably because no one has tried, but I did mention the six-year old who made the roses open.

Thanks to Drunvalo and others, we now understand how Jesus created his miracles, and how hard (or easy) it really is by going into the heart. My point is that Jesus may have been gifted at birth, but that's due to his hard work and experience in the past. It also took work to continuously maintain that skill once he was born.

Edgar Cayce did many readings for the people around Jesus. In all cases, their current personalities and jobs match what they were doing in biblical times. Very thoughtful people are social workers now. Very wise people then are still wise people now. Very bubbly people then are bubbly now, etc. Thus you carry these traits with you from lifetime to lifetime. Furthermore, if you are lucky enough to be immortal, then you even remember all the specific things you learned from your past incarnations.

Thus allow yourself for a moment to not think of Jesus as some holier than thou being that God sent here with all these special Terminator powers. Rather, think of Jesus as a goal of yours to become. The question then becomes, what type of personality would you need to be?

As an alternative question, who would you chose in the world to be the next Jesus? What are their personality traits? In my opinion, this is what really happened. Through dedication and hard work over numerous or even countless incarnations, someone was qualified and thus chosen to be Jesus. They passed the audition.

He or she may have waved their hand in class, or even dreamed up the concept of Jesus as a way of helping to solve the problems here on Earth. Who knows? Regardless, they needed to have the skills and dedication to perform the job at hand.

Keep in mind that it's easy to perform "miracles" on the higher levels. Your thoughts become reality instantly. (In golf, for example, holes-in-one get pretty boring after only a few!) The challenge is making that same miracle happen on the dense Earth plane. That's much more difficult. Remember Thoth created the Great Pyramid on a higher level and then built it (from the top down!) over a few days. The first part was easy. The second part is probably the result of many incarnations of dedicated practice and continuous improvement.

Thoth just happened to be at the right place at the right time (Atlantis and the Great Fall) - - and, more importantly, had the necessary skills to do the job at hand. Thankfully, he pulled it off. If he was not around at the time, would someone else have been able to create the Great Pyramid?

Thus, if I had to choose someone today, I'd choose Thoth to be Jesus. Hands down!

13.3 Who was Jesus - - Really

Thoth is a real person. He talks about his own father [4] and brother. He became immortal about 60,000 years ago. In the latter stages of that he was king of Atlantis for 16,000 years. His name was Chiquetet (which means seeker of wisdom) Arlich Vomalites [1]. Atlantis sank 13,000 years ago. About 6,000 years later he emerged in Egypt (during the Egyptian and Sumerian periods) as Thoth. He just sat there, observed, and wrote. His goal was to get wiser by simply observing everyday people and their struggles. (That what it takes - - studying - - just as if he were in school.)

He eventually left Egypt and re-emerged as Hermes in Greece [4]. This was about 2,500 years ago (well after Akhenaten and 500 years before Jesus). It was at the end of this Greek period that he wrote the Emerald Tablets [1]. One of the chapters is entitled "The Key of Wisdom", and that title pretty much summarizes what the Emerald Tablets are all about. It also emphasizes what Thoth was about. His life's goal was to become wise. That's a lot of life at 60,000 years!

Much of the above information is from the Emerald Tablets - - written Thoth himself when he was Hermes in Greece roughly 500 B.C. These are twelve hidden tablets, written on an indestructible material. In 1925 permission was finally granted by the Ascended Masters to allow ten of the twelve tablets to be copied and released to the public (why now?). You can buy those books today [4]. You can also search the web and see actual photographs of the original engravings by Thoth.

More recently, Drunvalo had contact with Thoth over about ten years (1984-1991) via meditation. Thoth revealed lots of historically missing information [1], especially regarding Atlantis, Egypt, and Sacred

Geometry. Although no names were mentioned, Thoth revealed he had "several different names" since Hermes. Thus Thoth was around us in relatively recent times since 500 B.C. - - since he wrote the Emerald Tablets.

Thus you have now heard Thoth's own words via the Emerald Tablets, and Thoth's own words through Drunvalo. Now let's move on to Edgar Cayce.

Edgar Cayce himself had a major prior incarnation as Ra Ta. This is incredibly significant. He, Thoth, and a third named Araragat were the three Ascended Masters who stepped up to the plate [1] to save us after the Great Fall, which was roughly the same time that Atlantis sank. As you know, Thoth created the Great Pyramid (as he states in the Emerald Tablets[4]), but the other two were still quite instrumental in the Big Fix.

One of the three Wise Men, named Aklar, brought the gift of incense to Jesus. Aklar, in turn, learned from the teachings of prior Persians named Zend and Uhjltd. Per Cayce, he himself was Uhjltd in a prior incarnation, and Zend was Jesus in a prior incarnation.

Cayce also confirms that the Melchizedek in the Bible was indeed an earlier incarnation of Jesus.

Thus Jesus indeed had been on Earth before. Per Cayce, Jesus also showed up in the 1919 meetings at the Geneva Peace Conference (of course he was inconspicuous) that ultimately led to the United Nations [Link 1302]

There's more, but most relevant here is he states that he (Cayce) knew Hermes when he was Ra Ta [Link 1302] and that Hermes also was an earlier incarnation of Jesus.

Connect the dots here, and it says that Jesus was Hermes, was Thoth, was king of Atlantis, and was Melchizedek, to name a few. This means that Jesus has been with us all along, throughout most or all of our history, and most importantly since the Great Fall 13,000 years ago.

This implies that Thoth and Jesus are one in the same.

Allow this possibility to be in your mind, if just for a few seconds, and it all makes perfect sense. If Jesus is our "Father", then Thoth is our "Daddy". He's done a remarkable job of taking care of us through this

Great Fall dilemma. If you think of him as a corporate QA Manager, he has stuck with us through all of this craziness, and has tried over and over to make things happen, unselfishly, on our behalf. His 60,000 years of wisdom, and his seeking continuous improvement during that time as an individual, certainly makes him my #1 candidate for Jesus. Unity consciousness is what he is.

So What?

Even if it's not actually true that Thoth became Jesus, it's a very suitable proposition. Thoth, or someone much like him, is my candidate for Jesus.

Thus if you simply set aside all the holier-than-thou aspects of religions, and think of the Great Fall as something that needs to get fixed, then it's a problem that needs to get fixed using the resources at hand.

We, your basic humans, are simply too ignorant to even understand the problem, much less the solution. It needs to be solved on a much higher level. There are indeed higher levels, which again we are too ignorant to understand, that have been working on this problem for thousands of years.

These higher levels have tried their best to get our attention and help us understand. This includes Egypt and Sumer and Greece, to name a few. Most recently this has been via all the new technology, the Jesus miracles, Thoth's recent communications with Drunvalo, etc., but we still don't get it.

You have to give all of these parties many thanks for all the efforts, not to mention the patience, they've endured. We are like mice running back and forth in a maze, and they are, I'm sure, quite frustrated - - and probably more accurately, quite fascinated (or something else that Spock might say in Star Trek).

Regardless of who your candidate for Jesus may be, one thing is for sure: the Big Fix has not been a one-man job. You have the original Big Three (Thoth, Ra Ta, Araragat), the Essenes and Akhenaten, and Jesus. There are many more behind the scenes as well as countless more in plain site (the indigenous tribes and those who placed the crystals, for example.)

All of these are in unity consciousness.

They simply want us to be the same.

That's a win-win for all.

Chapter 14

- Loose Ends -

14.1 The Marketing Plan

We've pulled back the covers a lot in these lectures, and I hope you've allowed yourself to see what's really going on. Per Cayce, Thoth returned as Jesus. Ra Ta, who was also there supporting us after the Great Fall, came back as Edgar Cayce.

Cayce performed "miracles", just like Jesus, and captured the world's attention as well. They were just different types of miracles. He was able to read the Akashic Records, whereas Jesus was able to magically create stuff.

Cayce also came at a time when many of the people around Jesus were being reincarnated. Thus it's likely no coincidence that Cayce showed up when he did. I also wonder if these people were intentionally reincarnated as a group.

The third Ascended Master who was by our side at the Great Fall, i.e., Araragat, has probably performed such tasks as well - - I'm just not aware of them. We do know that he went to Tibet following the Great Fall and the Flood. (We'll cover Tibet later.)

In addition, these individuals have, or probably have, returned in other settings as well. Some were proactively planned, and some were incidental. Perhaps Drunvalo's contact with Thoth was the latter, i.e., Thoth seized the moment that Drunvalo presented during a meditation. Who knows?

Regardless, the goal of all these events is to slap us in the face and wake us up. Each of these incidents is simply their way of "tapping new markets", i.e., reaching more and more people to get them aboard the airplane.

It's my opinion that the arrival and teachings of Jesus is just one of the products created to attract and train the masses. All of this takes work. There are no holier-than-thou shortcuts. The miracles performed are really not miracles at all. They just appear such. They take work and practice.

14.2 The Hebrew

There are a couple of very interesting loose ends that we'll now cover. One is the Hebrew.

I grew up in small town America and went to a tiny school. I was not until later in life, when I interacted with New York City, that the "Jewish issue" came into my realm. Exactly like the "Egypt issue", the Jewish issue was equally a head-scratcher for me. Why is this such an issue worldwide and throughout history? It's always been in the forefront, but there has never been a root-cause explanation.

Finally, thanks to Drunvalo/Thoth [1], I got an answer. It goes back to Atlantis, and you are going to have to stretch your imagination. It involves Sacred Geometry.

As explained earlier, the Adam and Eve population was on the Pacific land mass called Lemuria. Regular earthly events sink a continent here and raise another one there. Turning this problem into an opportunity our "corporate leaders" created Atlantis on this newly formed, uninhabited continent. In the United States we created Washington DC in a similar fashion. We first designed the city (streets) on this huge tract of vacant land, and *then built* the buildings.

The newly formed Atlantis was not concerned about streets. It was instead designed around the Tree of Life, and each of its ten circles was a city. The population was then split up, and each person delegated to live in a specific city-location, depending on their spiritual evolutionary status. There was even a wall splitting Atlantis in half, giving it left-brain/right-brain characteristics, and the only persons allowed on both sides were the few Ascended Masters.

The Cities of Atlantis
arranged in
A Tree of Life Pattern

A problem they faced was the population was mostly "female" (That's because we were finishing up 13,000 years of "female" on the Precession of the Equinox). Therefore, some of the cities on the left-brain could not be filled.

This is where the Hebrew come in. Where they came from is not important, but the Hebrew got permission to occupy two of the remaining four cities. According to Drunvalo/Thoth, the Hebrew wanted to "repeat 5th grade" in order to fix some details regarding their own spiritual evolutionary path.

Regardless of these details, and any missing details, for me this explains the Hebrew, but there is still a critical missing piece regarding the "Jewish Issue". This is discussed further below.

I presume the Hebrew are "older souls" than the rest of us, and thus understandably got upset when Jesus appeared as "the new kid in town". How would you feel if a new young step-dad came along and took over the entire household? Likewise this may also explain the "Star of David", i.e., that the Hebrew were familiar with Sacred Geometry prior to their arrival here.

14.3 *The Bad-Guys*

After the Hebrew joined us, the bad-guys (who had been patiently waiting and watching) saw a fabulous opportunity to leverage themselves. Thus, *without permission* they took over the final two circles in the Atlantis Tree of Life, and the rest is history.

As explained earlier, these bad-guys are perhaps the result of another Lucifer-type experiment that went terribly wrong. They are totally "male" and total sociopaths with no remorse whatsoever. There are only about 50 of them, but due to their selfishness (and they are quite intelligent), they control our banking system, military, religions, etc.

To pull back the covers even more (on what God is), I'll share with you some of the technology these bad-guys have (stolen from us is the more accurate statement). You are already familiar with the Bermuda Triangle. This is the location of one of their experiments that went terribly wrong - - creating the Great Fall about 13,000 years ago [Link 101].

They have a time machine. In 1942 the U.S. Military made a ship not only disappear (the goal was to make our ships invisible to enemy radar), but it accidentally and suddenly became 1985 for the two crew members who were "smart enough" to jump ship during the aborted test. Once they "arrived" in 1985, these two met up with their exact same "boss", but he was older then and had actually perfected the time machine. He sent them back to 1942, and instructed them to throw the power switch on the ship. It worked. Everything was correctly turned off, and they returned home. Listen to the very end of this link [Link 1401] for the story as told by one of these crew members. Also see [Link 1402]. Hollywood went a step further and made a movie based on this called "The Philadelphia Experiment".

My point here is the bad-guys now have selfish access to this time machine. I know of one other instance where it was used - - spur of the moment, and impulsively, by a good-guy for a good purpose. Nonetheless, you can only imagine what a great tool this is for the bad-guys to remain in power. For example, just think about elections.

They also have Star Wars technology. Airplanes did not bring down the World Trade Center [Link 1403]. Those buildings turned to dust, and literally floated to the ground. There was no seismic thump when they hit the ground. Instead there were huge pulses in our magnetic poles when each of the three buildings suddenly, and separately, started to collapse. Analysis of the dust revealed that the atoms had been physically changed from, say, aluminum to zinc. This is alchemy in the historical sense - - people trying to make gold from other materials. Normally, this only happens inside of stars at 10 million degrees. Explosions and fires can't modify atoms; they can only modify molecules - - which are made up of atoms. Thus these building were brought down by a Directed Energy Weapon (analogous to a laser beam) that tapped the 7.23 cm "free energy" of the universe, and changed the atomic structure of the atoms in the World Trade Center - - oh yes, and only the door handles of the nearby cars...

14.4 Modern Day "Jews"

About 600 B.C., the Hebrew were exiled to Babylon, and that is when the bad-guys starting infiltrating the Hebrew culture with their own custom-made belief system [Link 1404]. They replaced the ancient Jewish Encyclopedia with the Talmut, and the Pharisees became the leaders of the overall culture, completely redefining the religion to suit themselves.

Jesus was fully aware that these were the bad-guys - - the same bad-guys that we are up against today. He bitterly denounced them stating that they have made the Law of God of non-effect:

- - - - Matthew 7:13 - - - -

"Making the word of God of none effect through your tradition, which ye have delivered: and many such like things do ye".

™ ™ ™ ™ ™ ™ ™

If Jesus is indeed Thoth, you can imagine his rage more so. He brought the original Hebrew into this world, much like bringing in an adopted child, and now their lives are being used by the bad-guys.

- - - - John 8:44- - - -

"Ye are of your father the devil, and the lusts of your father ye will do. He was a murderer from the beginning, and abode not in the truth, because there is no truth in him. When he speaketh a lie, he speaketh of his own: for he is a liar, and the father of it."

™ ™ ™ ™ ™ ™ ™

In 70 A.D. the Romans destroyed Jerusalem, and the Pharisees gained even more power as the traditional Jewish sects, such as the Essenes and Sadducees, disappeared. In 135 A.D. all Jews were expelled from Palestine via a mass migration to Babylon, led by the Pharisees. Most of the Jews were already in Babylon from the earlier exile. Babylon was then recognized as the capital of Judaism. The Talmut was conveniently created, and it flourished for the next 1000 years under the Pharisees.

On the brink of the Crusades, about 400 A.D, Khazar warriors from Turkey conveniently invited themselves into the Jewish faith to avoid having to choose between the Christians or Islam [Link 1405]. These were very bad people, employing rape and pillage as their modus operandi. These people are the roots of the Khazarian Mafia which operates today out of Israel.

The true Hebrew people today are totally independent of this invasion. Unfortunately the general Jewish population today seems to pay the emotional price for the acts of these few really bad Khazarian Mafia bad-guys.

14.5 Pulling Back the Covers on God

Unfortunately, I had to give the bad-guys some press. However, it demonstrates just how much we have accomplished -- time machines, free energy, and this scary Star Wars weapon. There's plenty more, and there are good-guy stories as well. These are all based on pyramid technology, i.e., Sacred Geometry, and are of the same exact nature as your chakra system, the Consciousness Grid, the Great Pyramid, etc. This type of design is what taps the 7.23 cm energy.

I've told you these for a couple of reasons, but primarily to help get you out of your box and realize just how much we have pulled back the covers on what God is -- since biblical times. Had the Earth blown up between 1942 and 1985, the soldiers would have seen "no Earth" on their time-machine arrival in 1985, yet it would still be there once they returned to 1942. Such is a sneak preview as to what Earth itself really is -- a perceived reality. We are now even accepting the idea that there are multiple universes.

The above technologies, and things like Atlantis achieving an advanced culture via their city design, makes the Lucifer Experiment a little more tangible for us to grasp. For example, it is not much different from a time machine. Remember the 3 primary chakras, i.e., survival, physical contact, and then the terrible twos (ego)? I'm proposing that Lucifer, in his "lab", inserted that 3rd chakra, i.e., the ego; he inserted the 3rd piano note, which is where we are stuck now (Is this why is there no black note after *our* piano note?); he may have even inserted the Earth itself, which is the 3rd planet from the sun. If he did not actually insert the Earth, perhaps he chose the Earth because it was already the 3rd planet out, thus fitting his "math" appropriately. Who knows? Nonetheless, he did create our entire reality.

Is this where the term "As above, so below" comes from? This is a common phrase in spirit science. It is in the Emerald Tablets. It is in the Bible. It could imply, for example, that the spiral pattern of the galaxy is the same that of a hurricane, same as water going down your sink, as electrons swirling in the atom, etc. The above Lucifer example is another good example. Did his changes go all the way to the atom, then DNA, and all the way to the highest forms of the universe? Is this what the Bible means when it says "On Earth as it is in Heaven"? These are just questions, yet they prompt you to sit up in your chair and wonder - - in all kinds of directions - - including who or what is God.

14.6 The Prophets

If we are pulling back the covers on God and the Heavens, then we are also inherently pulling back the covers on "prophets".

What is a prophet? A prophet is simply someone who's been made aware of our future by the good-guys and who's *also* been given permission to share that information with you and me. It is not difficult for the good-guys to see into our future. That's modus operandi. Rather it's dangerous and unsuitable to share that information with the general public because we are not of unity consciousness and will typically abuse that privilege with our egos.

Thus prophets are not everyday people like you and me. They are generally more advanced souls who, once they are born on Earth, are given this information and trusted to treat it with care. They speak the truth, yet that is typically different from what the existing belief systems are, and thus they are shunned and often killed. Such is the case with Jesus as well.

14.7 The Jesus of Religions

Let's now get back to the debate about "Who was Jesus?" Is he the son of God? Is he the son of Man? Is he a prophet to Mohammed? Is he is a Jewish prophet preparing the world for God's apocalyptic overthrow of the evil forces. Is Jesus represented in Buddha?

To answer this question, you simply have to look up the definition of religion. Religion is defined as a *certain belief system*. Thus, with this definition in mind, Jesus represents ALL of these, and probably many, many more - - depending on your specific religion.

--Hebrew

Regarding the "apocalyptic overthrow" view, the evil forces could be the bad-guys, as well as the Lucifer Experiment. The Hebrew population definitely inherited the bad-guys after joining us on Atlantis. Depending on where the Hebrew came from, the Lucifer Experiment could have been a new experience as well. Thus it's no surprise that they might view Jesus as their savior from these issues, and band together to protect themselves. Per Drunvalo, all that "evil" will vanish upon the airplane taking off.

--Muslims

Muslims consider Mohammed to have restored Arabia to the unaltered and monotheistic faith of Adam, Noah, Abraham, Moses, Jesus, and other prophets. Thus, Muslims consider Jesus a prophet to Mohammed. Mohammed was born roughly 500 years after Jesus, and was visited by the Angel Gabriel. Gabriel made many such important visits throughout the biblical periods, and there is certainly no reason for him to stop - - even now.

--Hindus

When Atlantis sank, some of the more advanced beings, including Ra Ta, went to India and Tibet. This is why these regions employ the technical aspects of chakras, yoga, and the like, as part of their spiritual practices. Furthermore (fasten your seat belt for this one), the Earth has its own chakra system (as does everything) and with that comes its own sexual behavior (chakra #2). This is called the kundalini energy and is often referred to as the rising serpent. Each of us has the same. The kundalini center of the Earth has been located in the Himalayas (Tibet, nearby India, etc.) for the past 13,000 years. This is the reason some key Atlanteans migrated there.

Thus, just like San Francisco seems to be the "wild and crazy" place in the USA, this Tibet area is the wild and crazy area of the world for these practices. As a result these practices became more pronounced over time with some people spending their entire lives sitting on mountain tops, whereas others became more engrossed in the sensual aspects. The Hindus today fully endorse Jesus, yet Krishna is a god-like character who is playful, a model lover, divine hero, and Supreme Being. The latter simply means that God is everything to everyone.

--Buddhists

Buddha was born 400-600 B.C. (no written records until centuries later) in the Himalayan foothills in India. Thus Buddha came along during the above "wild and crazy" era, and simply said "Slow down, and let's find some mutual ground here that everyone can relate to". He was more of a leader, and not some self-proclaimed prophet or god. Buddhism is non-theistic, i.e., there is no physical God. Instead, you obtain unity consciousness by striving to be perfect, and not to get wrapped up in materialism or in the woes of your physical body and life's daily letdowns.

No one knows where Buddha came from, i.e., is he one of Thoth's buddies, just an everyday person, etc. However two things are interesting to me. One is the date (500 B.C.) corresponds to the date the Essenes first appeared (Akhenaten's re-emerged immortals). Could Buddha be one of them? More interesting is that Buddha really did not make any substantial changes. To me this implies that Thoth & Co. realized that things were relatively OK in that part of the world. Also recall that Jesus traveled there to study. Per Cayce, Jesus also lived and died there following the resurrection.

--Christians

Christianity is the Pauline belief system. These are the writings and ministry of Paul/Saul, who first met Jesus briefly after the resurrection. Per Cayce, Saul may have also been present when Jesus (age twelve) fascinated the Jewish leaders arguing spiritual matters.

Saul had been a harsh critic of Jesus and his teachings. Following the resurrection, Jesus decided to turn this problem into an opportunity, and he thus appeared to Saul in a puff of smoke. That turned Saul around, and he began his writings and teachings, and changed his name back to his original Greek name - - Paul. Paul was very naturally talented at statesmanship, i.e., getting the word out. He worked tirelessly into his sixties.

In the meantime, the Romans also turned a problem into an opportunity. They endorsed the Pauline doctrine and made it the "official" religion of the empire, an empire that was struggling to deal with all the religious branches stemming from Jesus' popularity. Paul, who was Jewish, also provided a convenient political link to Judea, which was not in Roman hands at that time.

———————

The Pauline doctrine is exactly that - - Paul's views. Paul believes that Jesus is "the son of God and he died for our sins". Keep in mind that Jesus himself made none of these claims.

Jesus demonstrated the power of the chakra system by performing all the miracles and healings. He also promoted the schooling that you can achieve the same. Each and every one of us has that power within us. It's fueled by unity consciousness and the realization that we are all one big working machine. Religiously, this is being "One with God". This is what the 2012 transition is all about: it's about us being in our hearts, and recognizing the power of the heart, i.e., the power of your own chakra system.

--The Rest of Us

Sinning is the everyday result (threat) of duality consciousness (free will). Jesus came here intentionally to die and resurrect. This embedded the resurrection recipe in the Akashic records - - so that each of us can still go to Heaven (the next dimension) even though we are not of perfect unity consciousness - - and regardless of what religion (or none) we stumbled upon,

However, another such event has taken place. Recently (after 2008) about 6000 Ascended Masters ascended from Earth onto the new grid and then beyond. Some intentionally returned. This was a practice run on the new grid. It worked!

Thus exactly Like Jesus' mission, this "trip" stored that information in the Akashic Records - - establishing the new grid as a viable pathway.

Not only that, it established the new grid as the pathway for the rest of us. This assures, for those of us unable to actually ascend or resurrect, that we can still make it onto the new grid.

The next chapter provides *those* instructions.

Thank You !

Tom Price

- Getting Aligned -
For the Planetary Transformation

Part IV: Getting Aligned

- CHAPTERS -

Chapter 15

- Getting Aligned -

We've spent a lot of time on the airplane analogy, i.e., getting us on board, the luggage discarded, and now we are awaiting flight attendant instructions. The pilots have the all-clear from the control tower (the universe).

This chapter is what all the prior chapters have been leading up to: the Fibonacci growth-event (the quantum leap) that's required to graduate us from the 3rd up to the 4th dimension. This chapter is those flight attendant instructions. It is the instructions for you to Get Aligned.

As you already know, many third parties have done their part to get us to this point. - - and - - just like the airport ground crew gets everything ready at the last minute for takeoff, the same is true here.

Thus this chapter reveals not only what you need to do; it also reveals what these third parties have done at the last minute to help everything Get Aligned as well.

What do we need to do? The answer lies in asking the right question. To do that, we have to go back to our beginning, which is Adam and Eve, and then fast forward to the latest point in time where everything was OK and doing just fine. That was during the good times on Atlantis.

Recall that the Adam and Eve gang were initially relocated to Lemuria and given permission to flourish. A Priesthood emerged there. The indigenous Maori people, currently in New Zealand, are that original priesthood.

Keep in mind that the Adam and Eve gang were created with permission, and this implies that the "corporate world" is committed to helping us flourish and achieve higher and higher levels. Thus, there is a whole hierarchy above the local priesthood. They are not operating alone.

Then Lemuria sank, Atlantis rose, and thus began the new and improved Adam and Eve gang. Recall that Atlantis was arranged in a Tree of Life pattern. A revised priesthood emerged on Atlantis. That priesthood is the Mayans, now of Central America.

These priesthoods are depicted by the rings below:

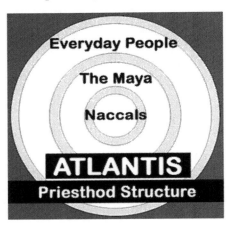

You and I are the outer ring, the everyday people on Atlantis. The Mayans are the intermediate ring.

The innermost circle (the Naccals) is very advanced. Today the Naccals are the Kogi and Arawak people in Columbia and South America, respectively. They live at very high elevations, deep inside mountainous caves. Those mountains are like pyramids, focusing the energy of the universe. As a result, the Naccals are constantly levitated (floating off the ground), and they glow a greenish hue. They are connected directly with Mother Earth and the universe at all times. They are of pure unity consciousness.

The Mayans are the priesthood, i.e., the link between the Naccals and the everyday people. The Hopi Indians of the Southwest are also part of that original Mayan priesthood. When they go into meditation or ceremony, that's when they are connected to the Sacred Place of the Heart (which you will learn more about below). This allows them to connect to Mother Earth and everything-everywhere.

When Atlantis sank, roughly 13,000 years ago, all of these tribes got into boats and rowed to the locations where they now reside. There are a handful of other tribes, scattered all around the world.

They and their indigenous priesthoods go back tens of thousands of years, and they are very much alive and practicing on our behalf today. They are performing the same important ceremonies just as if we had been with them on Atlantis the whole time. They have never forgotten us. The problem is we've forgotten them. We have completely forgotten that we lived on Atlantis. We have completely forgotten the Atlantean priesthood. We have forgotten ceremony. We have completely forgotten our ability to live via the heart.

To get us all "aligned" in the airplane, the ancient world and the modern world need to get synchronized once again.

The Key question is:

What would we be doing now on Atlantis had the Great Fall not occurred? That's precisely what we need to be doing now - - today. Thus, it's finally time to set religions aside, lean back, and open your mind and heart to the ancient wisdom. Put yourself there once again.

15.1 Mayans Have Taken the First Step

In July 2007, a Mayan elder, and leader of the 440 councils representing the Mayan tribes in Central America, showed up at Drunvalo's house in Arizona. He knew Drunvalo, and knew him to be the key figure in the world capable of bringing the right people together at this critical time.

He explained [Link 1601] that the window of time has arrived, on either side of the 2012 date, to bring the world together in ceremony - - the first time in 13,000 years. Based on the Mayan past experiences, he explained some of the physical phenomena that would occur on Earth. More importantly, he explained that there is roughly a 10 year window of time, and the 2012 events could occur anytime during that window. They were also waiting for a certain cosmic warning sign, which had not yet occurred, to better define that window.

He also explained that the entire world needs to participate (This is the alignment step that I've been talking about), and the Mayans needed to get the word out to you and me.

This is the first time in 500 years that the Mayans have said a single word to the outside world. You can thus appreciate how serious this is to the Mayans, and therefore how serious it is to you. We need to connect with the Mayans and the ancient world. We need to connect via our hearts and our knowledge.

Jesus emphasized the heart, and the Mayans are emphasizing both the heart (how) and their ancient knowledge (what). These are connecting via both the "female" and "male", respectively, i.e., a complete connection. Likewise the Mayans and other indigenous cultures need to understand us and our modern knowledge of the universe.

15.2 What Do You Remember from the Ancient Times?

What do you remember from the ancient time?

Nearly all of us, when we go on vacation or even weekends, often seek out Mother Nature. Do you ever wonder why? What is it about Mother Nature that draws us? It gets us away from using our minds and more about using our hearts. I am not talking about petting your dog or cat. This is about really connecting with Mother Nature in that mystical way.

I've noticed that it takes me a solid week of vacationing to "forget it all". Then, when I come back to the rat race, in that first day or so, time itself goes by incredibly slowly. I'm still on "island time". Why is that? What is that? It's because you are still thinking with your heart, and not your mind. Your heart does not know time.

You've also heard of incredible stunts, like mothers lifting cars off their children after an accident. How can that happen? Such miracles happen when we discard our brain (mind) and think only with our hearts. Our hearts are very powerful. We lost that trait, and our memory of it, in the Great Fall. This example demonstrates that we still "got it". We just need to give it water and sunshine.

Geronimo, the famous last-stand Apache of the American Southwest Indians, was able to avoid the Calvary for so long because he used this power of the heart. You can cover incredible distances with no food or water.

In the book *The Quest* [2], Tom Brown brings this into modern times. He is taught (1962) by an Indian shaman in New Jersey to, among other things, jump into ice water and sweat. Likewise, great distances are covered with no food or water.

⸻

What's above are examples of the power of the heart. This 2012 transition requires you to re-learn this ancient habit that all of us have, but have forgotten thanks to the bad-guys and the Great Fall.

The indigenous tribes, however, have maintained that ability and, as you read below, it is very powerful.

15.3 Ceremony and Mother Earth

Many ceremonies have been performed specifically for this 2012 event. What is a ceremony? What happens during a ceremony?

It's all about a certain vibration (energy, frequency, whatever you want to call it) in your heart. The Mayans and all indigenous tribes are in this heart vibration all the time. They are not simply on island time and sloughing off. They are very much aware, very much connected, and fully understand the power of the heart - - exactly like Jesus. Specifically they are living in the Sacred Place of the Heart.

When the Mayans asked Drunvalo and his worldwide representatives (of all religions, etc.) to come and do ceremony, this was to connect the hearts of everything everywhere. That's all of mankind, Mother Earth herself, all the animals, the plants, and everything else on Earth. It also includes "Father Sky", which is everything else above, including all life everywhere in our universe. All of these objects were originally created via the Flower of Life manifesting the energy of our universe. Thus, believe it or not, all of these objects have a chakra system and a heart chakra - - and most notably the Earth herself. They are alive.

Those ceremonies connected all of these systems, and especially Mother Earth, via that common thread, i.e., the heart vibration (that certain frequency). At the peak of these ceremonies, everything is vibrating at this same frequency, and the goal is to increase the volume (amplitude) sufficiently to achieve the required result. That's why the eagle sat motionless for ten minutes overhead [Link 102]. You can call that a miracle or "weird" if you choose, but it's really the result of this vibration and the associated multi-participation ceremony. The eagle was participating as well. So was the wind. So were the trees. The Mayan elder would simply lift his hand, and the wind would blow through the trees time and time again.

Several ceremonies needed to be done - - with the Mayans representing the ancient world and its priesthood, and Drunvalo & Co. representing the modern world and its priesthood. Both needed to be represented, just as they would have been (on Atlantis) had the Great Fall not occurred. Incidentally, one of these ceremonies included a water-sprinkling baptism [Link 102].

These ceremonies have not been performed in 13,000 years. That's the schedule. This is extremely serious business because, in timing with the 2012, another important page (cycle) was being turned in the history of our 7.23 cm energy-driven cosmos. Turning that page requires a unified effort, i.e., a unified heart vibration of all.

There have been other important dates in these 13,000 years, and the Mayans (and other indigenous tribes) have successfully done the required ceremonies. Thus we have to thank them for their continued hard work and commitment.

For 500 years, the Mayans have never shared anything with the public. Now for the first time in 500 years, the Mayans want the public to know.

That, in and of itself, should get your attention. This is why these lectures were written.

The Mayans are our original (Adam and Eve) priesthood and existed long before Jesus, the Bible, or anything else. They would very much be a part of our daily lives - - today - - had the Great Fall never occurred. Jesus would likely not be in our vocabulary had the Great Fall not occurred.

Thus we have to put all of our differences and egos aside, and respect our relationship with these ceremonies and what they represent. This is above and beyond the Great Fall and the Big Fix. This is above and beyond the Bible and Jesus' mission. This is our innate connection with the universe and Mother Earth. Most importantly, it's recognizing that success was achieved by using the heart.

The next step is watching these videos, reading the books, etc., and educating yourself on the ancient world, i.e., understanding and appreciating what they have quietly done for us the past 13,000 years. Respect our relationship with the Mayans. This respect goes out to all indigenous tribes.

15.4 *Mother Earth & Father Sky*

Notice how much Mother Earth is appreciated through all of this.

The Druids (Celtics of England) were yet another offshoot of Akhenaten's immortals [1], and that group was started the same time as the Essenes - - about 500 B.C. They were very much into nature and greatly respected the creative processes of Mother Earth. Heaven for them was inside the Earth, and that is where you went when you died. Thus Mother Earth was indeed their Mother, and the Sun was their Father. Both were very much alive to them.

Jesus visited the Glastonbury area of England on several occasions with his uncle, Joseph of Arimathea. Glastonbury Abbey was subsequently created on land proactively donated by the Druids.

The Druids had many sacred sites. Sixty four of these were stones circles, and the exact centers of those circles were (GPS-wise) on a straight line which ran across England exactly consistent with the Grid's ley lines. Christianity came along, in a bigger way much later, and built churches over their sacred sites. The Christians placed the altars of those churches on those exact GPS coordinates, and encouraged them (stated politely) to look upwards towards God and Heavens - - instead of down into the Earth.

Before all this was Akhenaton. He got the Egyptians (who were confused by that time) re-focused onto one god, and his was the Sun. He intentionally kept it simple.

Through it all, the indigenous tribes around the world have existed and worshipped both. They don't really worship, but rather connect with both Mother Earth and Father Sky as an essential part of meditation and ceremonies. I've repeatedly stated that everything is based on Sacred Geometry and the piano. Could these be what "Mother Earth" and "Father Sky" also represent? Sacred Geometry is the physical things and shapes that manifest in our world. The piano is the energy waves, i.e., the non-physical aspects of our existence. Thus by connecting to both the physical and non-physical aspects of our existence, these indigenous cultures are connecting to everything, everywhere as part of their meditation and ceremonies.

However, the more day-to-day logistics are that Mother Earth needs to be specifically acknowledged (and therefore Father Sky represents everything else). That's because we are inherently tied to Mother Earth via the Consciousness Grid.

This all sounds high-tech, yet it's what the indigenous tribes, not to mention their more advanced hierarchy of immortal beings, have known all along. If you go back to Adam and Eve, that's two hundred thousand years. That's a lot of experience!

Yet behind this "technology" is still, as the indigenous tribes call it, "The Great Spirit that moves in all things", which remains that evasive creative force "which we don't understand", yet greatly appreciate as God.

Jesus also emphasized our connection with Mother Earth (Nature). The next section might help reinforce why.

15.5 *Mother Earth Has Done Her Part*

Recall from Chapter 14, during the Hindu discussion, that the Earth's kundalini energy has been located in Tibet. It's been there for 13,000 years. As of 2012, and right on schedule with the Precession of the Equinox, the kundalini moved. It moved from the Tibet area, apparently meandering here and there around the globe, and finally settled into the Andes (Chile) in 2002.

(A similar shift is happening now, and it's in the news. That's the magnetic pole shift. "Kundalini" is a strange-sounding term for what is nothing more than a comparable shift. Are these a match pair?)

This is a huge event, and the indigenous tribes were bustling with activity to acknowledge and welcome it.

According to the local tribes, it was indeed there, but according to Drunvalo (who visited the area a few times) something was amiss. It seemed blocked or restricted - - for a few years. Finally he got a call from the indigenous tribe on Easter Island to please bring his counterparts and do ceremony. They were aware that a major sin (cannibalism) needed to be repented. They also needed to do a ceremony that had not been done in 13,000 years [Link 102].

As this latter ceremony was being completed, an amazing golden light came down from the sky, mid-day. Drunvalo asked if they had ever seen such before, and the answer was no.

After they had barely finished, another unexpected call came (from Tahiti) saying that Earth was now giving birth, and *another* ceremony is urgently required.

Tahiti is exactly opposite the Great Pyramid and, much like our own backbone, the Earth's chakra "backbone" runs between these two points. Interestingly, Tahiti is a heart shaped island, with a heart-shaped coral reef around it. Humans give birth at the lower end of their backbone. The same is true for Mother Earth. This is where her "baby" was coming out.

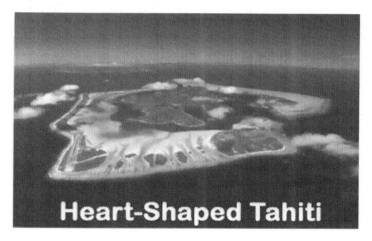

Heart-Shaped Tahiti

In a panic, Drunvalo & Co. rushed there from Easter Island. After arriving, and a nerve-racking three day delay to get to the exact location within the island, the ceremony finally took place. The seemingly pointless delay was because Drunvalo thought he needed to be at the exact center of the island. The queen, who was his host, did not have jurisdiction over the center; instead the very old king did. Once the king met Drunvalo, and he had to so within inches because of his poor eyesight, he knew immediately that Drunvalo was the right person. Drunvalo, on the other hand, realized then that the king had a very huge heart - - consciousness-wise. The king sat on his plastic chair at the beach and joined the ceremony. At that point Drunvalo realized that he hadn't even planned the ceremony, as he'd been all tied up with the logistics. After a brief meditation, he had his party members collect natural items reflecting air, water, and earth. He arranged them in a Sacred pattern on the beach (Later, the king commented that this is exactly what he had in mind), and the ceremony was successfully completed.

Those who stayed on the island afterwards for a couple of days got a nice surprise when they revisited the ceremonial site the next morning.

A starfish-shaped light had appeared on the sand directly over where the ceremony had been [Link 101]. There were plenty of joyful tears at that point. The birth of the new Grid had begun. It now had life. This was 2008.

Three weeks later the ceremonial art had washed into the sea, but the light was still there, floating on the surface.

Incidentally, on the night just before that ceremony, Drunvalo got an urgent letter from a colleague in Australia stating that a lunar eclipse was occurring the next day ‐ ‐ the exact day they were doing the ceremony.

Like most reefs in the world, climate change has weakened or destroyed them. The same was true in Tahiti. Drunvalo had brought his son there to see those beautiful fish, but there were none. About two weeks later, Drunvalo got a call from the king, stating that the beautiful fish had returned to the reef.

───────────────

After returning home to Arizona, Drunvalo got the calling, through meditation, to do yet *another* ceremony. Once again the troops came from around the world. As that ceremony was taking place, a (completely unexpected) lunar eclipse occurred at their exact location in Arizona.

Drunvalo scratched his head (and, more importantly, meditated) for many days, and finally put together what all these events and lunar eclipses meant. The unexpected Easter Island event, as well as the nervous three-day delay on Tahiti, were the Ascended Masters' chosen technique for coordinating the date - - delaying the Tahiti birthing ceremony so it coincided exactly with the first lunar eclipse.

The actual birthing of the grid, like having a baby, takes 29 days. This was bracketed by the lunar eclipses. The latter eclipse is the day the grid finally was fully born

Thus Mother Earth's preparations are done.

Everything is now set for you and me.

This was February 2008.

───────────────

Remember the Essenes? Remember how diligent they were about making sure all the prophecies (including astrological signs) were fulfilled? This is a perfect modern-day example. As a minimum, it's proof that everything is somehow linked - - the Earth, the Sky, everything. The Essenes knew. The Wise Men knew. Jesus knew. The ancient world knows.

The ancient world now knows that everything is in place, and they are simply waiting on us.

15.6 The Ascended Masters Have Done Their Part

Recall, from the end of the previous chapter, that 6,000 Ascended Masters ascended from Earth onto the new Grid and beyond. Some intentionally returned. This was the "practice" run on the new grid.

Let this all sink in. This is a *synthetic* consciousness grid that we've built over the past 13,000 years. Just like building a car in your garage, we just took it out for its first test run. There is no difference. There is no holier-than-thou aspect to this at all. It's the result of pure hard work and commitment.

Meanwhile, this whole "thing" is built for you and me, and we don't have a clue.

The Mayans are now banging on our door and saying "wake up, wake up"!

15.7 The Fibonacci (The Final Hurdle)

Recall from Chapter 3, when the discussion was about giants and the heavens, I provided strong mathematical evidence that our 2012 transition is indeed a Fibonacci event - - as it should be if we are governed by the Flower of Life. Drunvalo also independently emphasizes the Fibonacci in his video *The Mayans of Eternal Time* [Link 102]. This is the video he made on behalf of the Mayans to encourage us to get involved in this transition.

Recall the sneezewort plant. It looks back into the past and sees the "5". It adds to it the current "8", and then it knows to make 13. (Note that this applies to both the leaves and the number of branches.)

That's what the sneezewort plant does, as well as many other things. The relevant question is what do you and I have to do? We are humans, not plants, and our Fibonacci growth is quite different.

What's happening to us is probably best demonstrated by the atom, and specifically about the electrons orbiting around the nucleus. Electrons can have only certain orbits. When you excite the electrons (by heating the material to a very high temperature), the electrons absorb that energy - - and they speed up. Eventually they'll get enough speed (stored energy) to jump up into to the next higher orbit.

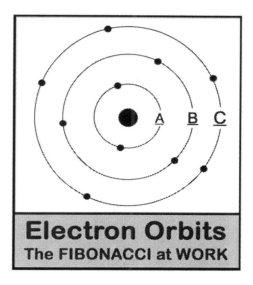

Electron Orbits
The FIBONACCI at WORK

The interesting thing is the only "allowable" orbits are those of A, B and C as shown above. There are no orbits in between. You can choose to be totally confused by this - - or - - you can immediately recognize that this as a Fibonacci situation. It's a quantum leap from one state to another. The electron absorbed energy until it had enough to jump to the next higher-energy state (the next higher orbit).

Although physicists don't recognize it as such, and have all kinds of fancy math to describe it, this is nothing more than a Fibonacci event - - based on the Flower of Life. You are now an expert in quantum mechanics! I nearly flunked the college course because the quantum mechanics approach to this was so difficult to grasp.

Whereas the sneezewort plant is concerned about adding leaves and flowers, you and I are concerned about our bodies absorbing energy and thus vibrating at a higher state. We are exactly like the atom!

You can also choose to think of it as our DNA absorbing energy and jumping to its next higher Fibonacci state. This is, perhaps, the most suitable way to think about it. We are simply growing. Recall how teenagers seem to put on sudden massive height-growth. We'll experience a similar jump in growth, but that growth will be in the frequency of our vibration. With that comes the ability to create "miracles", and with that comes less dependency on the physical world around us for survival. (This is the "female" arriving, and the "male" becoming less important, respectively.) And yes, we will also have a substantial increase in our actual height (Recall the heights of the Egyptian Statues in Chapter 2), but since we can create "miracles", we can make ourselves appear to be anything we want. Most people choose to be the beautiful person they always thought they were.

Now you know what is going to happen. The next question is *how* is it going to happen?

Recall the 7.23 cm energy that's all around us. That's the E-note on the piano. To understand the 2012 event, simply imagine that the 7.23 cm energy suddenly increases to the frequency of the F-note. Your body has to be able to absorb that higher energy. Once it absorbs it and stores enough of that new energy, then "poof"- - you will jump to the next higher state. You will then be in the 4th dimension. You will indeed be of a "higher vibration".

Whether or not you agree with this electron analogy, everyone agrees with the bottom line - - which is that you have to be ready to receive this higher frequency energy. You have to have a receptor. You can think of this as a TV satellite dish. Recall from Chapter 1 that the Holmdale Horn Antenna was a receptor that absorbed the energy of the Big Bang. This is essentially what you have to create within your body.

Figure 16-1. Your Heart Chakra is the Receptor for Receiving the Higher Vibrational/energy.

Once the receptor is there and working properly, then that energy will inherently be received.

Everyone also agrees, and this includes Jesus, that this receptor is your heart. It's your heart chakra. It's the same heart chakra (and vibration) that was used in all the ceremonies by Drunvalo & Co. It is the same heart chakra vibration in which the Mayans, and all indigenous tribes, seek to be in all the time to connect with Mother Nature. It is the same heart chakra vibration that all of us would be using, had it not been for the Great Fall. It is also the same heart chakra and vibration that the bad-guys have worked diligently to keep us ignorant about and inept at its use.

15.8 The Bottom Line

Thus learning our "past" is about re-discovering the power of the heart chakra, how it applies to the 2012 situation, learning how to actually use it, and then actually using it to get successfully through this transition.

You just gotta do it!

You have to be of unity consciousness because unity consciousness is what creates that heart vibration within you. Think of it as a light bulb. It needs to be on, yet it can be quite dim. Then, when that energy shows up, you are indeed ready to receive it and take that breathe. It then glows that much brighter.

If you are not of unity consciousness, then that energy just goes wherever. Like a lost grain of sand on the tone-plate (Chapter 2), you'll hop around a bit before you are finally back home in the stable Flower of Life pattern. This means that will ultimately catch up to the rest of us, as did the grain of sand. Meanwhile you'll go to what is commonly called the astral plane, which is where you go now in between reincarnations. There you will deal with your ego-luggage (your sins) until, once again, you are given the opportunity to be of unity consciousness, to learn the power of the heart, and to rejoin the rest of us.

As the Mayans have stated, there is no fixed date. There is instead a window of time.

There is also no Cinderella complex regarding this transition, i.e., you have to make this happen via your own free will. We all do. That is what determines the ultimate date. Drunvalo has been working for 30+ years to bring us and the ancient world together. Many others have done the same. Jesus promoted the heart and unity consciousness. Many others have done the same. Now the burden is up to you and me.

As President Franklin D. Roosevelt said "You have nothing to fear but fear itself". That is very much the case here. Unity consciousness inherently takes away those fears.

The remainder of this chapter is instructions to help you further achieve unity consciousness, to help you discover and/or further discover you heart chakra, and to get you more familiar with our ancient past.

Following this, we talk about the importance of meditation - - a brief technical discussion. Chapter 17 continues this by addressing different audiences, and how they can reconcile their own belief systems against this necessity of going into the heart.

15.9 So What Do You do Now?

Here is a quote from Drunvalo on this matter [Link 1601]

"Our ancestors still exist in their old form. They hold knowledge that is so old we don't even know that it exists anymore. And yet we can't go on, i.e., ascend to a higher level of consciousness, without knowing that information.

We have to connect with them. They know they can't leave without us. They have to have the information we have, and we have to have the information they have."

- - - - - - - -

Here is a corresponding set of instructions to help you get aligned:

1.   Recognize that all religions were created as a result of the Great Fall. Thus, let's put all of our "differences" and egos aside and respect our relationship with the ancient world, which is our common link.

2.   Recognize that the Mayans are the "Keepers of Time", as well as our ancient priesthood. Their timely ceremonies and daily wisdom have kept us aligned with Mother Earth and synchronized with the universe.

3.   Understand and appreciate what the ancient world has quietly done for the past 13,000 years, and what they want us to know now at this crucial time. This is above and beyond the Great Fall and the Big Fix. This is above and beyond Jesus' mission. This involves our innate connection with the universe and Mother Earth. In their language it's the innate connection with Mother Earth, Father Sky, and the "The Spirit that moves in all things"

The two most comprehensive videos are [Link 101] and [Link 102]. These are full length documentaries, 1 ½ - 2 hr each. The former is our history, including the Great Fall and the Big Fix. The latter is the Mayan perspective on current times, and the things they want us to know.

4.   Body, Mind, and Spirit are equivalent to Father Sky, Mother Earth, and The Great Spirit, respectively. Ditto for the Father, the Son, and the Holy Spirit. To learn more, revisit Chapter 1.

5.   Practice or, better yet, live unity consciousness (This is "Love" as discussed in our section on Consciousness, Faith, and Love in Chapter 16). Unity consciousness (Love) can be objectively thought of as service to others, knowing this goodness will come back to you. Different religions have their different ways and means of teaching unity consciousness. Follow your heart, and practice the techniques which are most meaningful for you. You want to feel that vibration in your heart.

For example, in Jesus' terminology, "Do unto others as you would have others do unto you". If you have no religion, and are a materialistic business owner, then treat your employees as you would want them to treat you. Treat them as if you were one. If you prefer meditating on mountain tops, then do that. The point, however, is to do it. Do it consciously. Have your alarm clock go off to remind you, if necessary. The more you do it, the more your awareness goes up, and thus you reach a higher level of consciousness - - and a new reality. Use the 51 percent number as your guideline: Spend 51 percent of your time and/or 51 percent of the things you do living and promoting service to others, the universe, and Mother Earth. Your intentions count. This should be your goal. Chip away at it.

6.   Remind yourself that ancient technology is 200,000 years old, if not billions of years old. Everything is alive. You are far more than just flesh and bone. Mother Earth is far more than just dirt and rock.

As a result, your intentions count far more than you may realize. It's perfectly fine to be sitting next to Jesus and the Mayans on the airplane. If you are comfortable with Jesus and Thoth being the same individual, then you are sitting with the Mayans and the king of Atlantis, just like ancient times. Get comfortable. Make that your intention.

7.   Proactively recognize Mother Earth by doing the Unity Breath. The Mayans (and other indigenous tribes) recognize Mother Earth and Father Sky, and have each of them acknowledge you back during your meditation. At that point, the three of you are one with spirit. Your intentions make you aware that there is a real connection and results in a certain vibration. This, in and of itself, is a good, easy, tangible practice. See the book *Living in the Heart* [4]. Here is a guided meditation online [Link 1503] by Drunvalo. It's optimum to do this outside, in the sun, with your body in contact with Mother Earth (e.g., barefoot).

8.   From there then go into the Sacred Space of the Heart. Jesus did this as part of his ritual to perform his miracles. This, too, is in the book *Living in the Heart.* This requires a strong commitment. Nonetheless, just reading and understanding it is a powerful reminder of the ancient world's wisdom. Here is a guided meditation online [Link 1504] by Drunvalo - - the male way. Here is the identical meditation, but the "female" way [Link 1505]. Try both - - and this goes for males as well. As a minimum listen to these and understand them.

This really demonstrates the difference in "male" versus "female". It is so much easier the female way. This means that miracles are so much easier the female way. That's where we're headed.

Meditation is very important. Any meditation is good because it acknowledges that there's more to life than just our physical bodies. Any meditation is good that encourages capturing the energy of the universe and transmitting the Love (unity) consciousness. Any meditation is good that encourages that Love consciousness manifesting into our beautiful, healed, loving Mother Earth and her inhabitants.

A beautiful Mother Earth is where we are headed, no doubt, so this is a good thing to visualize with our unity consciousness.

If your belief system needs a Heaven, then simply visualize the next dimension as such for Mother Earth and her inhabitants.

On a technical note, it's important to realize that you are creating that initial higher vibration even though your light bulb might be quite dim. To understand this, recall the energy diagram from Chapter 1.

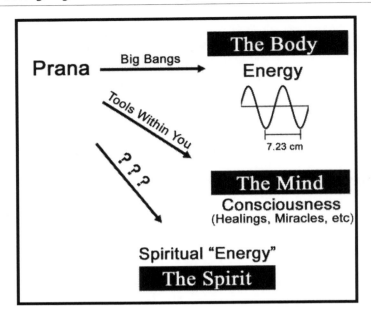

Figure 15-2. Consciousness comes from Prana, and not from the 7.23 Energy of the Big Bang

It states that the 7.23 cm energy comes to us from Big Bangs. That is not the case with consciousness. Within your body, you have chakras, and they (and not big bangs) convert that Prana into consciousness.

Thus you have to use the heart chakra within your body to create that required higher vibration (that higher piano note frequency). It is your job to create this from scratch.

Once you "get it going", this higher vibration becomes your receptor, and you then get more and more of it.

This is like push-starting your car or hand-cranking a lawn-mower. Once you get it going, it takes off by itself. The key point here is you have to be the one to initially convert Prana into that higher vibration.

You do this by consciously creating unity consciousness. If you are good at it, then you do it by being in the Sacred Place of the Heart. In the latter case is you go right the heart, and essentially turn the key (no push starting required). This is how it is with indigenous people, and especially the shamans.

If we were all in the Sacred Place of the Heart, the airplane would have taken off instantly and a long time ago. This could have been the case on Atlantis had the Great Fall never occurred. It could have been the case today if we were all Mayans. However, we have forgotten this knowledge. That's the primary problem.

Now, thanks to Drunvalo and others, millions of people in the world are doing very advanced meditation techniques to help us through this crucial time. Those are the first class passengers.

For the rest of us, who are (humorously) stuffed into the coach section of the airplane, it's really a matter of commitment and intention, rather than difficulty. Your intentions count. You light bulb can be dim, but it does need to be on. That is what "Getting Aligned" means.

Chapter 16

- The Awakening -

The prior chapter on Getting Aligned gave you some ideas and direction for practicing your part of the Fibonacci. A later chapter on Different Audiences will provide additional insights and ideas. These are the things you do on *your* end of the telephone line.

This current chapter on Awakening reveals what's happening on the other end of that consciousness telephone line, i.e., who's listening and how.

First, we give you a better feel for how the universe changes day to day, i.e., over time. In a sense, that's creation. We'll then cover actual events that are happening right now, so you can see for yourself.

16.1 How the Universe Works

The universe does not use a compass and a straight-edge to create itself, but rather it's based on fractals - - which create a hologram. Modern physicists and spirit scientists often agree that we are in a holographic (fractal-based) universe.

Here we provide a quick tour of what all that's all about.

First, let's introduce the fundamental building blocks of our universe. The rudimentary "bricks" are the circle and the equilateral triangle.

Once you choose a fixed circle that also fixes the size of the corresponding equilateral triangle. This combination is, therefore, a single fundamental building block:

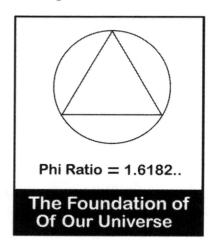

Phi Ratio = 1.6182..

The Foundation of Of Our Universe

Recall that Sacred Geometry is always drawn using only a compass and a straight edge. It's fascinating that, by using these exact same tools [1606], the above shape yields exactly the Fibonacci Ratio of 1.6182. Recall that the Fibonacci sequence determines the quantum rate-of-growth for the items in our universe.

Thus, the circle and the equilateral triangle define our universe. This single shape is the fundamental building block of the Flower of Life. It determines the Fibonacci. It is the fundamental building block of Sacred Geometry itself.

However, what I've shown you so far is the two-dimensional version (something you can easily draw on paper). It is actually a *three-dimensional* object, and here is *that* scenario:

If you insert another equilateral triangle you get the Star of David shown below.

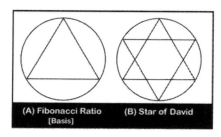

(A) Fibonacci Ratio [Basis]   (B) Star of David

More importantly, in the three-dimensional view, you get a star tetrahedron.

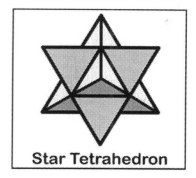

Star Tetrahedron

Now imagine this star tetrahedron encased in a sphere.

The Fundamental Building Block
Of Our Universe

That pair (the star tetrahedron & sphere) is the true building block of our universe. It is the three-dimensional version of the circle and equilateral triangle.

Let's now "turn on" this machine. Let's "turn on" this fundamental building block.

That takes energy. We need to talk energy.

Recall from Chapter 1 that the universe has a constant source of energy (Prana). Recall that many people properly argue that prana is not energy, but instead it is the life-force. Please use whatever concept is comfortable for you.

The star tetrahedrons are what plug into that energy, making it available to you. These are your chakras.

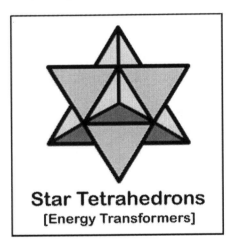

Star Tetrahedrons
[Energy Transformers]

Star tetrahedrons are the transformers which capture the universe's energy and convert it into a usable form - - consciousness. Jesus could not have healed, created miracles, or resurrected without his. (In some cases you can get away with a pyramid, which is half of a star tetrahedron.)

In the figure below, the very first star tetrahedron (B) taps the energy of the universe, and generates the Flower of Life (C) which is also called the Seed of Life, the Egg of Life, and the Genesis pattern (just the circles).

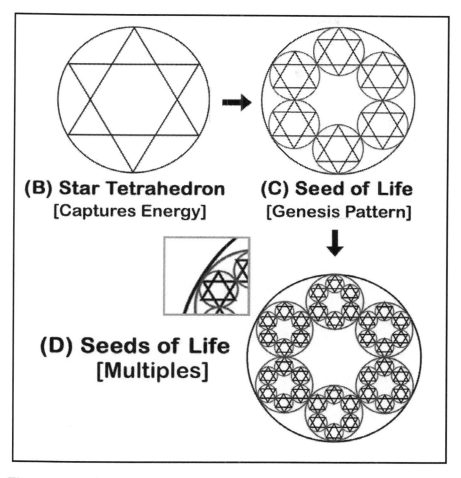

(B) Star Tetrahedron
[Captures Energy]

(C) Seed of Life
[Genesis Pattern]

(D) Seeds of Life
[Multiples]

That energy was also used to create the star tetrahedrons located within each circle (sphere). Thus there are now multiple fundamental building blocks in (C) created by the single building block of (B),

Now, we simply repeat that process: Each of the six star tetrahedrons in (C) taps the energy of the universe to create the Flower of Life in each of *those* circles - - creating (D).

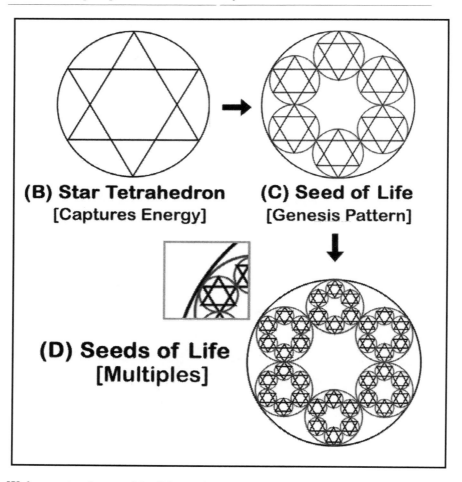

(B) Star Tetrahedron
[Captures Energy]

(C) Seed of Life
[Genesis Pattern]

(D) Seeds of Life
[Multiples]

Welcome to the world of fractals, i.e., repeating patterns that make a whole. That is what holographic means. Everything reflects everything else. Everything is reflected in everything else.

Let's back up before you scratch your head too much. Recall our Lucifer conversations. I proposed that Lucifer, in his "lab", inserted that 3rd chakra, i.e., the ego; he inserted the 3rd piano note, which is where we are stuck now (Is this why is there no black note after our piano note?); he may have even inserted (or at least chosen) the Earth itself, which is the 3rd planet from the sun. The point is, whatever he did on one layer, that exact same change was done on ALL layers of our universe, on all the fractals layers of what we know as reality. It really cannot be otherwise in the world of fractals.

You can go as small as you want. Just as important, you can also go the other way. You can now, perhaps, grasp the Big Bang more so. From a pin-point, it just exploded into larger and larger fractals.

There are zillions of star tetrahedrons in your reality - - some are tiny on the sub-atomic scale and others are massive - - like black holes. This includes the planets, which are the chakras (star tetrahedrons) of our living solar system.

Now you know why it's called Sacred Geometry - - because it creates this fractal design with the energy-capturing star tetrahedrons. It creates our entire universe. Just one little thing has to be changed and then, "poof", everything changes - - from the atom to Mother Earth and beyond, i.e., the entire universe as we perceive it. (The bad-guys were likely, and illegally, attempting one of these "poofs" when they accidentally created the Great Fall.)

All of this is invisible to you and me (e.g., you can't see your chakras). Recall that, at each of these star tetrahedrons, other mechanisms, based on Metatron's Cube, determine the physical shapes of the objects which you and I actually see. Metatron's Cube is all the straight lines, i.e., it is the "male" aspect of the Flower of Life.

All of this is invisible to you and me (e.g., you can't see your chakras). Recall that, at each of these star tetrahedrons, other mechanisms based on Metatron's Cube determine the physical shapes of the objects which you and I actually see. Metatron's Cube is all the straight lines, i.e., it is the "male" aspect of the Flower of Life.

If you put on your "star tetrahedron" glasses, analogous to night vision glasses, all you will see in our universe are the star tetrahedrons and their associated energy field pattern.

Is this where the term "as above, so below" comes from? The spiral pattern of the galaxy is the same as that of a weather system (hurricane), same as water going down your sink, etc. In a sense these are indeed fractals of one another.

Now, most importantly, you have a peek into what is going to happen (technically) when we ascend, and why everything (including you and me) is going to go at the same time. This is what 2012 entails; it's one of these "poofs". It's not the end of time, nor the end of the Mayan calendar. It's just a new reality, and that includes a change our concept of time. Physically, imagine that your DNA going through a Fibonacci step change.

At the same moment, Lucifer's duality consciousness will be replaced with unity consciousness. This is a catch-22 in a sense because we need to achieve unity consciousness in order for this change to manifest. That is our challenge. This, too, prompted these lectures.

Artists Note: This is for those who are closely scrutinizing the above figures. We stated above that item (C) was the Flower of Life. Closer inspection reveals that the six small circles of (C) need to be twice their size to truly represent the Flower of Life. If we drew it as such, and continued accordingly with (D), (E), and (F), then these figures would be a confusing mass of overlapping circles and star tetrahedrons - - because it is a 2-dimensional depiction of a 3-dimensional shape. We chose to simplify it for the reader's sake.

16.2 Consciousness, Faith, & Love

Think of your star tetrahedrons as a light bulb, and your consciousness equates to both how bright it is (magnitude) and what color (frequency) it is.

Ceremony is simply various parties coming together and generating the same frequency - - thus creating a much more powerful (magnitude) signal.

This, in turn, is what "Getting Aligned" for the Fibonacci event is all about. Everyone on the planet needs to be generating that frequency - - at the same time.

The more tuned up your chakra system is, the more (prana) energy you capture, and thus the more energy you generate. Practice make perfect.

"Service to Others" (unity consciousness) increases the brightness of your light bulb. This is precisely why Jesus taught us "Do unto others as you would have others do unto you".

The ancient world wants us to know and acknowledge their wisdom. Thus, if you are providing "service to your neighbor" and at the same time acknowledging the wisdom of the ancient world, then give yourself credit for helping both worlds at the same time. Your light bulb is then putting out twice as much. Visualize it more so as helping your family and friends, and that's even more energy. Feel free to multiply your efforts in this manner. Your intentions really do count in this manner.

━━━━━━━━━━

Faith is simply knowing that what you want to happen will indeed happen. There is absolutely no doubt in your mind. When you combine faith with clear goals (prayer, affirmations, etc.), then the signal (frequency) you generate is crystal clear. It's exactly like a high quality radio signal versus a poor one.

A book I wanted to write a couple of decades ago was totally faith-based. It had three main points:

(i)   Having faith and associating that with crystal clear goals (clear signal generated),

(ii) Giving and treating others like yourself (unity consciousness) which multiplies the magnitude of that signal, and

(iii) Giving thanks: Recognizing that there is something or someone out there listening and helping you – regardless of what your religion calls it. This acknowledgement keeps you open (it's your ears or antenna) for receiving incoming signals.

These points are the common basic recipe of all religions, and thus all religions work. If you don't have a religion, that's fine. You simply need to know these rules, or their equivalent, and operate accordingly.

Advanced meditation techniques are nothing more than these same rules, but you are exploring more so *how* these rules work - - thus refining your methods on a more scientific basis. You become a professional. Ascended Masters, such as Jesus, are masters at this. "This" is Love, i.e., the spiritual definition.

This "Love" is what the Fibonacci is really about. This "Love" is what Jesus taught. This "Love" is the energy. It's what creates the magic and the miracles.

Now let's discuss that magic.

16.3 The Aspen Event

In August 2013, Aspen Colorado experienced high radiation levels from a single Fukushima-contaminated rainfall. The government freaked because it meant removing about a foot of soil over a huge 100 square mile area, not to mention the trees, etc.

At least a couple of scientists had hi-tech Geiger counters [Link 1602], and those scientists are the source of this information. On about the second or third day, when everyone thought it was all over for them and their children, the radiation miraculously vanished - - over a period of about three hours in the middle of the night. It then went to unprecedented low levels.

Did Mother Earth herself fix this? I don't know. Did someone use a time machine to fix it? Probably not - - because the levels now much lower than the original baseline. Was this the result of pure consciousness, like Jesus turning water into wine or little girl who opened the thousand rosebuds? Could it be the result of crystals [Link 1603] much like those used to fine-tune the grid? These are simply questions. Is this the one and only time events like this have happened? Probably not. People just happened to have fancy Geiger counters in their houses to clearly document this particular event.

We have pulled back the covers a lot on what God is, and something like this Aspen incident is definitely within the realm of being achieved by pure consciousness.

From my perspective, this Aspen event gives you a glimpse of the 2012 transition we are currently going through. Once we get ourselves sufficiently aligned, then "poof". Just like that, our entire reality could be transformed.

16.4 How is it Going to Happen?

Recall the 7.23 cm energy. This is all around us. That is the E note equivalent on the piano. This transition is all about going to the F-note (4th dimension) and ultimately to the G-note (5th dimension). The G-note is the real "Heaven". It is the highest dimension on which there is still some semblance of a physical body. Since you are mostly energy, it's easy to imagine, and therefore change, your reality. You body changes into whatever you want, so everyone chooses to be beautiful. Your house is whatever you want. You don't need food. You don't need gas. If you want to travel somewhere, you are just there. If you want to be in the biblical Heaven, then you're there.

The challenge is we have to get from here to there - - safely. That is what ascension does; it gets you from here to there. The Great Pyramid was practice for exactly this. The problem is we have lost all of those skills. We don't have a Great Pyramid in our back yards, and we don't have Akhenaten to train us.

The Fibonacci is about us collectively generating enough consciousness to make this happen, but what's going to happen on an individual basis? What's going to happen to you during this actual transition?

Here we provide those answers.

If the E note has a 7.23 cm wavelength, then the F-note has a shorter (higher energy) wavelength at 6.82 cm. If you simply ratio these numbers, that's a 6% increase in energy.

The best analogy I've come up with is jumping onto a moving train. You first need to get your speed up. Then you jump onto the moving train. You can then relax. You just successfully caught the 6.82 (faster moving) train. You are now in the 4th dimension.

Another analogy might be pulling the chord to start your lawn mower engine. You have to put in some energy of your own to pull the chord on that new 6.82 engine. After one good pull, the motor is up and running and you are in the 4th dimension.

A similar analogy might be push-starting a car. You have to put in the energy to get it going 6% faster. Once you reach that target speed, the engine starts and runs on its own.

Note that in all of these analogies, you have to put energy into the effort. It may be a small amount (like pulling the chord on your lawn mower) but, nonetheless, it requires free will on your part and at least a little bit of effort.

———

Where does the energy come from for that "little bit of effort"? Where does the energy come from for your share of the Fibonacci?

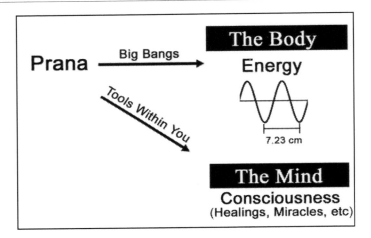

It comes from you using your mind to convert the prana into consciousness. It comes from meditating and generating (listening to) the G-note in your heart. It comes from you raising your vibration. It requires your active participation.

16.5 *When Will "It" Happen?*

The Mayans themselves have publicly announced a window of time [Link 102]. They base it on a prophecy which indeed occurred. That was a comet which exploded into a huge blue display, bigger in the sky than our Sun. This happened in October 2007 (Comet Holmes) just three months *after* the Mayans first contacted Drunvalo to bring his world entourage to begin the Precession of the Equinox ceremonies. That sighting launched a window of time that ends about December 2015.

Other indigenous tribes, respectfully, have their own warning signs and predictions. Nonetheless they all agree that we are due now for major earthly events associated with the Precession of the Equinox.

The Book of Revelations (in the Bible) is more of the same. The warning signs, instead of being stars and comets, are instead details of what's happening all over the planet at that time.

I've mentioned the book The Quest [2]. In this book a Lipan Apache shaman did a vision quest in the early 1900s. A vision appeared that had three warning signs. The first was "a disease born of monkeys, drugs, and sex". The second was "holes in the sky", which I presume are the ozone holes. The final sign, when it's too late, is "the night of the bleeding stars" and a blood red sky thereafter.

Although such predictions get our excited attention, I personally do not want to address this "when" question. That's because no one really knows the answer, including the Mayans. They just know that they have been "right on" every time for the past 26,000 years. Likewise, the Book of Revelations was written 2000 years ago. It needs a serious upgrade. I'm certainly not a prophet. Such predictions are really best left as simply more questions.

I especially do not want to address this "when" because the events now are so unusual, even to the Mayans. I'm talking about the Great Fall, the Big Fix, the devastation via the bad-guys, the planet being ruined, etc. These are not every day events in the universe. Under normal circumstances, "2012" (Precession of the Equinox) would have come and gone, and we would have (most likely) ascended as residents of Atlantis. This would have been a big deal, but a "normal" big deal.

However, in our case it's basically do or die. The Big Fix (fixing all the Murphy's Law items) *have to be completed* by this "2012" - - or never at all. We have to seize this opportunity. Thus, it's my opinion that "2012" will be delayed (if it can, and that is a BIG "if") until you and I are properly aligned for the Fibonacci.

———

Such dates and warning signs are a "male" issue. We like these because we can hang our hats on them. Others like such because it allows their ego to criticize such forecasts.

However, the "female" rules. This means that the "female" ultimately decides when and even how it happens. It does not have to make sense. This is precisely why the Mayans provide a window. They fully understand that the female is unpredictable.

———

Finally, the "poof" itself could happen over time (it might be happening as I write this), rather than instantly, and this creates yet another definition of "when". As the "poof" happens, we are able to change our own reality more so by our thoughts (our consciousness). That, in turn, can impact (what we perceives as) time itself and the actual events. This confusing feedback loop makes it that much more important to not worry about when, but rather simply concern yourself with the task at hand - - unity consciousness [Love) to make it happen.

The one thing we know for sure is the Grid is up and running after 13,000 years of work. We also know that modern physics and spirit science are finally coming together on how things work - - and that the Kogi in Columbia and those sitting on mountain tops in Tibet (these parties have fully understood what it's all about for eons) are likewise simply waiting for us.

You are in control of when.

16.6 *Mother Earth has Ascended*

People communicate directly with Mother Earth in their meditations. She's alive just like you and me. Per Cayce, we were supposed to have specific catastrophic changes on the Earth in 1998, just like the prior ones when continents rose and sank. That never happened. Cayce has never been wrong. Something is amiss. Furthermore, Cayce offered this on his own - - without being asked.

We were definitely not ready to ascend in 1998. The grid was not complete, among other things.

The consensus among Drunvalo and his contacts, with 99.9% certainty, is that Mother Earth has already ascended. She is in the 4th dimension. She is in "Heaven". However, just like Thoth created the Great Pyramid and then "lowered" it to Earth, the consensus is Mother Earth instantly changed our reality so that we remain in the 3rd dimension - - until we are more ready to ascend.

I know this sounds nuts. However, again recall that Lucifer created our reality. The bad-guys tried in Atlantis. The Bermuda triangle continues to do so today for the unlucky ones. The bad-guys have a time machine, etc. The good-guys have done things as well, and Mother Earth has done others. Thus, it's not crazy at all to imagine Mother Earth doing this. Per Drunvalo, it's easy for her to do so.

───────────────

Why is Mother Earth doing this? We've spent 8,000 years building and tuning up the Consciousness Grid. In my opinion, it makes no sense to have major Earth-changes destroy the Grid (by moving continents around) before we have the chance to use it.

Furthermore, we are getting more and more aligned. This includes, especially, the more advanced meditators - - who are being taught newer advanced techniques all the time. Those techniques are being taught "from above" exactly like the Ascended Masters taught Egypt and Sumer in the past. Likewise everyday people like you and me are getting more aligned all the time. This counts as well. It's all part of the required Fibonacci event. Mother Earth can't do that for you. Your free will effort is what's still required.

However, Mother Earth benefits from this as do others (including the 250,000 onlookers from other cultures). That's because we are all connected and part of the Whole. Remember the fractals. When we ascend, it is not just us in our little corner of the solar system. Our entire solar system ascends with us. The entire universe benefits. That's fractals at work. It really cannot be otherwise.

Thus our future timeline is up to Mother Earth. She's holding the cards. She's waiting on us.

But... what is she really waiting on?

16.7 Healing the Earth

Recall how an indigenous tribe or two had to repent. Cannibalism, human sacrifice, etc., were major sins (bad karma) that had to be dealt with before the Grid could be turned on.

What about us? There are seven billion of us that have all but destroyed the surface of Mother Earth and its inhabitants. This is major sin (bad karma) and, per Drunvalo, it has to be dealt with before we can ascend.

Could this be what Mother Earth is waiting on? This makes perfect sense to me.

Imagine waking up tomorrow, and a beach near you is suddenly thriving and full of vibrant colorful fish; The next day a forest near you have been miraculously replenished with trees and plants; The next day the a polluted river near you is magically pure and deep.

Can you imagine? The news will have nothing to talk about but all these miracles that are happening. More and more people will want to join the movement, and thus put in the effort to get better aligned. It'll catch like wildfire and grow exponentially. As all this happens, we'll not only have "repented" and fixed the Earth, we will approach the 160% energy that's required for the Fibonacci to occur, and then "poof". It does.

———————————————

Of course, no one knows if things will happen this way. For me it is a very viable hypothesis because it fits the "math" (160%) of the situation; it encompasses the required repentance (earth healings); and we've already seen such miracles happening today (thus it's believable).

Chapter 17

- Different Audiences -

Up to this point, the target audience in these lectures has been what I was - - a male brought up in a Christian environment who just couldn't blindly swallow all the clichés. However, my real target audience is everyone, everywhere. Hence, here I discuss several other key audiences.

17.1 Christians & Priesthoods

Religions have been an important lifeline over the recent millennia. Now it's time for religions to look in the mirror - - and get aligned with the heart chakra.

Unity consciousness is what Jesus taught. He was teaching you how to use your heart chakra. His miracles are proof that it works. That's why he performed them. He clearly states that *you can perform* miracles as well. Perhaps some of you have. All of you will. Jesus is very much alive and well today. It's time to remember what he taught us, and make him proud of you.

There is no Cinderella complex when it comes to such 2012 events. Jesus is not going to come and magically save us. Jesus himself never said he was a savior. Those claims are the result of the belief system created by the Pauline doctrine.

You and I are the "Little Engine that Could" instead of "There's something wrong with us, so we need help". We don't need help. We don't need a "savior". That power (our chakra system) is in each and every one of us. Jesus instructed us to use it. We just forgot about that system. We need to be reminded. We need a mentor, and that's Jesus and what he himself said and taught.

The math rules in such debates: the Fibonacci requires everyone, regardless of their religion or none, to create that higher vibration. This vibration is the same as "being One with God". It's all the same thing. It is a certain frequency, exactly like a certain frequency on your FM dial. We need to tune in and also turn up the volume.

The universe is simple. It has to be. There are zillions of self-help books that tell you how to create your own future, i.e., if you simply imagine your future correctly, then it just happens. Prayer works the same way. That's what's happening here as well with the Fibonacci. If we "imagine" the 4th dimension correctly, then it simply happens.

You can certainly imagine Jesus leading us like a shepherd leads his sheep, but we (the sheep) have to still climb the hills and cross the rivers. We need those skills, and it requires free will. Our chakra system needs to create that Love frequency. Jesus cannot do it for us.

It is also time to eradicate all fear associated with religion. Fear is detrimental, and fear-in-religion is a tool used extensively by the bad-guys to control us over the millennia.

17.2 *Children & Their Parents*

You (the children) are very powerful. Today 99% of the children being born are souls that have never been on Earth before [1]. Why? They have come to help. The "good-guys" got permission to bring in advanced souls, mostly 5th dimensional souls from Sirius, the Pleiades, and other star systems.

Most of these are in the same vicinity of the night sky, on either side of Orion's belt. Go out at night and look at the stars. Your real home is out there. Many children know this and blatantly tell their parents where they came from.

This started in the 1970s (right after our sun put out its first ever helium, rather than hydrogen, flare). In the past 20 years, 100% of the births have been of such souls. These kind (old) souls have volunteered to help Earth. Some are performing amazing miracles - - like the roses blooming. That's because they are already of unity consciousness. That's where they came from. Once they arrive here, however, it's hard for them to deal with our 3rd dimensional reality. They are used to simply imagining something and, "poof", there it is. They are used to being "tuned in" and getting schooled in an instant. Now they have to deal with eating, sleeping, poor parenting, and the ADD issues resulting from exactly that - - they are not interested in the stuff we teach them, and especially that in school. It's a tough world for them. Be understanding of them.

Why are they here? They are our major weapon against the bad-guys! The world population has skyrocketed from 3 to 10 billion since about 1970. That's a lot of new (old) souls! Billions of these children are here, including your own - - and possibly even you! We do not need to "teach these old dogs new tricks". Their chakra systems are highly tuned, far more than the rusty ones we (the older folks) have. They already know how to behave for the Fibonacci event. That is why they are here. They also learn advanced meditation techniques much more easily. This allows them to create the bulk, if not all, of the Fibonacci requirement. Thanks to them, the rest of us can likely just "coast" through it.

Some examples of these most advanced souls are the Crystal kids, the Indigo kids, Super Psychic kids, Star Children, etc. [Link 1604]. They are helping very much with all aspects of this transition.

By reading this I hope these kids feel more understood, and I hope the parents reading this will become more enlightened and educated about what's going on. Parents should fully encourage psychic development, spiritual development, unity consciousness, etc., to enable their children's chakra systems to work properly - - just like that of Jesus. Listen to the kids instead of the doctor. They have a lot to teach us.

The bad-guys are making their best attempt to thwart this effort by directly supplying drugs on the street, tainting vaccines, using the pharmaceutical market, reducing the population through diseases, etc. Aids is one horrific example. SARS is another.

All of us need to become aware, and all of us need to take action to protect and allow these kids and adults to flourish.

17.3 Atheists

Everything stated in these lectures is completely consistent with atheists' views as well. That's how it should be.

You can argue, of course, but we have totally pulled back the covers on God here to simply be the 10^{96} gm/cm3 energy that is present in the vacuum of space (the Prana). We can't explain that one or where it comes from. We just know it's there. With that, and some kind of a "spark", the fractal universe explodes into existence - - creating our reality of consciousness (which is zillions of star tetrahedrons glowing and interacting.)

Sacred Geometry determines how these star tetrahedrons interact, thus forming our universe.

From that point forward, it's individuals (such as Thoth & Co., Ascended Masters, Angels, etc., and even our neighbors in the cosmos) who are doing their very best to manage and tweak all the interacting energies to benefit the Whole - - to help us and to help us help ourselves.

Respect the Mayans and the ceremonies, as that is you and me doing *our part* to tweak things in order to benefit the whole. Go a step further and understand the chakra system, as that is the engine which enables you to do your part.

Standing around and doing nothing is just that. That is not an active Atheist. That is someone standing around and doing nothing.

Follow the basic Mayan instructions and keep improving. Connect yourself with Mother Earth and Father Sky, recognizing that you are all part of the whole. Unity consciousness is universal and is practiced by everything, everyone, and everywhere.

Get on board.

17.4 The Rest of Us

If you meditate, keep doing what you are doing, yet continue to improve. Meditation is the best thing you can do. Do the Unity Breath, go into the Sacred Space of the Heart, and then into the Tiny Space of the Heart. The latter is the true source-place of miracles. In all of these, you are using the heart to create that certain vibration.

Many of you perhaps don't meditate, yet feel a sense of awareness and connectedness (unity consciousness knocking on your door). That awareness is exactly what's needed from the masses. Follow the basic instructions, including the Unity Breath, and keep improving. Never stop improving.

Clear your mind and body of trash. Much like meditating, you get rid of (take care of) those things that keep you from having clear thought. Cleanse your body both mentally and physically.

Eliminate fear. Simply don't allow it to enter your door. Fear is a huge tool of the bad-guys. Almost none of the things we fear (worry about) actually come true.

--Children

Children, 12 years of age and under, will be fine. They know exactly what to do. Parents often worry about their children. Don't. It's the other way around. The children are the most talented in this regard, and that's why they are the ones performing the miracles.

--Women

Women are many moves ahead men in achieving unity consciousness. Do meditation, yoga, etc. Do the Unity Breath and the basic instructions. Simply get on a program and keep improving.

As stated above regarding your children, take the restrictions away so the children can flourish. Assume that everything has been tampered with by the bad-guys. This includes the air, the water (fluoride), medicines, the media, etc., - - to destroy these kids' ability to help spiritually.

--Men

Teach the men. Give them books like this.

The men are the most difficult because they are driven by the logical mind, and thus the ego gets in the way. We have been, since the Great Fall, in a world based on survival. The men have thus taken on the role of the provider, and that led to the mind being more important than the heart. That's a huge problem now at this time.

Things are turning around, thankfully, but there's no time to wait for that. Thus seek out male-based books and videos such this one, Drunvalo's "Ancient Secrets of the Flower of Life [1]", The Quest [2], and several of the provided links. There's plenty of bad-guy information on the web. Educate yourself as needed on the bad-guys, but then quickly forget it. That is not the answer as it's your logical mind and ego at work.

Switch the focus to the heart and the basic instructions we provide in Chapter 15 "Getting Aligned". Go out into nature and, when no one is watching, do the Unity Breath and listen to the natural sounds around you. They will talk to you.

You can also surround yourself with a ring of rocks and let only protective bright light in. Simple exercise like this change your consciousness, your awareness - - even if it is just your intentions. Never stop improving. Make that awareness your everyday awareness and your everyday goal.

Chapter 18

- The Future -

18.1 The Bottom Line

The universe, after all these discussions, is energy. That energy can decide to create. When that happens, it follows the laws of creation. The latter, stated in terms that you can now relate to, are (i) Sacred Geometry, (ii) the Piano (sine waves), and (iii) the Fibonacci. Everything, everywhere, is the corresponding blossoming of that energy via these laws.

Thus, our future is no different.

The universe (our fractals) is expanding, and will eventually contract, as part of its own sine wave behavior. What's relevant here is our universe is constantly changing (evolving) on all levels. We are part of, and have the responsibility of "keeping up" with, that moving target. You can think of it as growing up, and needing a new set of clothes now and then. This is why the Mayans have come forward. It's time to make a significant evolutionary move. A huge sine wave is beaconing us, and we are waking up to it more and more every day.

We don't need to think about the bad-guys as their world will simply crumble away (that's the fractals at work.) We just need to think about the Whole, and that's what unity consciousness (Love) does. Jesus taught this. He wanted us to observe this in nature, as well as in him, and then learn to do it ourselves. We need to connect to the Whole.

--What is the "Whole"?

The DNA of our universe is Sacred Geometry and the "piano". In a sense these represent the "Whole". Sacred Geometry is the specific physical shapes that manifest in our world. The "piano" is the energy waves and their specific frequencies that occur in our universe.

Other word-pairs can represent this "Whole" (everything, everywhere) such as Mother Earth and Father Sky, or perhaps Jesus above referencing "in nature" versus "in him"?

Sacred Geometry and the "piano", in turn, come from our even more basic DNA, which is the circle and its associated equilateral triangle.

We have not discussed this amazing fact: you can take that equilateral triangle, and by drawing Sacred Geometry straight-lines within, you come up with exactly the twelve piano note frequencies.

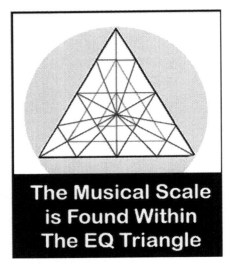

The Musical Scale is Found Within The EQ Triangle

Thus Sacred Geometry and the Piano are "the same". They are one thing. That's remarkable! The universe is that simple.

More so, and on the greatest levels of understanding, we are all one being. Our entire universe is one being. We came from the same singular Circle and Equilateral Triangle. We are all, and always, connected via the exchange of consciousness, much like the different parts of our body are connected and are one being.

Thus, that other person walking down the street is you, as are the plants, as are the planets. You are all one being, as are the rocks beneath.

This is how different people, audiences, and objects should be viewed. That is what unity consciousness recognizes. This is what unity consciousness, in essence, is.

Thus follow the provided instructions and focus on helping Mother Earth and Unity Consciousness [Love) achieve what we've been working on for 13,000 years. Then let's celebrate.

18.2 What is the Future?

First, it makes no sense to destroy the consciousness grid after eight thousand years of hard work. Thus, if major earth changes will occur (continents moving), then it only makes sense that this would happen during or immediately after the "poof". Thus you can let go of those fears.

In these lectures, I have not provided any specific futures. That's because the future is subject to change. Our own consciousness can change it.

Recall in Chapter 6 that I presented two different histories. I do not own a crystal ball. Thus I will do the same here and provide two different futures. Both are from extremely reliable sources. We'll then compare, and you can see the similarities.

--Scenario A

Scenario A is based largely on Drunvalo and the Mayans. It is the most likely scenario based on what you've read in these lectures.

In Scenario A this "poof" begins with the magnetic pole shift. The Hopis say that this will coincide with a momentary great increase in energy in each of us (as well as the planet). If you are of unity consciousness at that moment, then it massively grows (and becomes part of the Fibonacci). If you have fear, then that massively grows, and (per the Hopi) you die - - and go elsewhere for repair.

With that same magnetic shift comes thirty (30) hours of blindness, so do not panic. Simply hold hands and employ your unity consciousness to assure those around you that all will be OK.

Following that will be the actual pole shift (that Cayce talked about). This means the outer skin of the earth will be free to rotate (much like the shell of an egg). Continents will then be free to move, and they will. Massive earthquakes, volcanoes, rising and sinking continents, biblical flooding, etc.

Drunvalo is adamant that everyone will "make it", that the bad-guys will be gone forever, and we'll live here on beautiful Earth as the 4th dimension quickly blossoms into the 5th. The 5th dimension is the most Loving of all the dimensions, i.e., it's the real "Heaven".

The timing of this is determined by the 7-year window of the Mayans, ending December 2015.

--Scenario B

This scenario is directly from Gordon Asher Davidson in his book *The Transfiguration of Our World* [6]. This information is directly from an Ascended Master. They communicate telepathically during meditation. It continues today.

Per Gordon, the 9/11 attack was the "final straw". That's when the Ascended Masters got special permission to finally clean house and remove the 50 bad-guys off this planet (just like they got permission to build a synthetic consciousness grid). The bad-guys are gone.

The roughly 150,000 people and all the remaining bad ETS, who were selfishly living in the underground cities (this is the New World Order's hiding place while they destroy the rest of us via nuclear war, etc.) have also been moved to a different "dimension" as well. At least two of these underground cities (Colorado and DC) were recently destroyed by earthquakes. Thus, the message is clear: it's over for the bad-guys and their agenda.

Ascended Masters are now working directly with world leaders to promote and enhance change. As a result, bad-guy-associates are being removed from power, and changes are being made to the world's systems. Businesses and government will become for the people for the Earth, rather than for greed.

No earthly catastrophes will occur. Those events have been superseded by this "management" intervention.

An intense good-guy energy will infiltrate the planet, and those who are in unity consciousness (Love, which is "a certain vibrational frequency within you"), even somewhat, will be uplifted to the 5th dimension.

We will work together, and that includes the Ascended Masters, to promote a beautiful Mother Earth and her inhabitants.

Those who are selfish will not survive this intense energy. They will be shifted to the astral plane (where we hang out between reincarnations) and reside in environments compatible with their evolutional capabilities.

The Solar System itself is governing these events because it needs to make its own evolutionary move. Earth is holding it up, and we (thanks to the bad-guys) are holding up the Earth.

18.3 Comparing the Two Futures

In the big picture, these two scenarios are identical. The bad-guys are gone. Selfish people won't be around to interfere. Earth will return to its glory, and the people on it will live happily ever after. Virtually everyone makes it - - eventually.

The Fibonacci is a necessary event. Indeed both scenarios have intense energy hitting the planet, assisting this event.

The Ascended Masters could have eliminated the bad-guys anytime, but it was decided eons ago that they would be allowed to stay - - and essentially stretch the limits of Lucifer's duality-consciousness (free will) experiment. Both scenarios support this.

Both cases agree that Mother Earth has already ascended (Scenario B calls it "Nature").

Both scenarios are based on direct communication with Ascended Masters during meditation. That communication is no different than you and me talking today, and it's far more effective.

The difference is Scenario A respects the historical aspects (predictions) of the Mayans, Cayce, etc. Scenario B, however, reveals that the Ascended Masters now have permission to bypass all of that and "intervene" to make immediate changes - - essentially because the bad-guy experiment has run its course, and it is now time to move on.

———

What do you and I have to do to participate?

Both scenarios emphasize that "Love" is the answer, i.e., we have to generate "Love" to propel us through the Fibonacci. They can't do it for us. Thus, Getting Aligned remains your top priority.

Both scenarios strongly encourage you to inform others to do the same. It's a numbers game.

18.4 Transfiguration vs. Transformation

Scenarios A and B are essentially identical in the long term, but they are vastly different in the transformation actually occurs. In Scenario A, we have to ascend, resurrect, or (the rest of us) actually die. These processes then birth us into the 5th dimension. We then join back up with a beautiful Earth.

In Scenario B, however, we are not going anywhere. We are staying right here on Earth. Instead of us going to the 5th dimension, the 5th dimension is instead coming to us. No one is going to die. Instead we and the Earth will miraculously change as we live day-to-day. Thus Heaven comes to us instead.

This is carefully being orchestrated by the Ascended Masters, as it is very much an exception to the rule in the universe. You normally have to die. This is why Scenario B is termed the "Transfiguration".

The changes will occur at a rate that we can handle.

That rate, in turn, depends essentially on how fast we become aware and aligned.

18.5 Is Jesus Coming Again

Per Gordon in Scenario B, the answer is yes. Jesus will return. He will show up waving the checkered flag once this transfiguration process is well underway.

My guess is that it will be Thoth regaining the "throne" as the King of Atlantis he once was. That's because the Great Fall is repaired and we are finally back to where we belong, the bad-guys are gone forever, and the "female" in each us will rule with a big heart - - just as Jesus taught.

Amen

Chapter 19

- Epilogue -

Now that you've been educated on the Sacred Geometry of our universe, you can finally grasp that the Dark and the Light are simply the different humps of a sine wave. It's all part of the math.

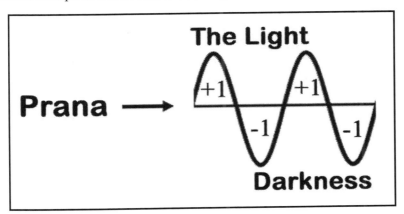

Thus the Dark is *supposed* to be there. Here is a biblical reference to that.

19.1 Satan (the Darkness) is (manifested as) The Bad-Guys

- - - - Ephesians 6:12 - - - -

"For we wrestle not against flesh and blood, but against principalities, against powers, against the rulers of the darkness of this world, against spiritual wickedness in high places."

Paul is saying that the darkness has its own beings (presence) that naturally inhabit other dimensions. Per both Drunvalo [1] and Gordon [6] the uppermost level of the bad guys is indeed beings of another dimension, and not physically here on Earth. Our Duality Consciousness experiment presents a great opportunity for them to have a seemingly "wicked" agenda.

Free Will (Duality Consciousness) dictates that both the Light and the Dark forces will be tugging at us, being equal and opposite. However, the Light always wins (in the long run).

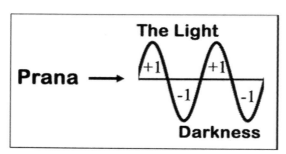

That's because our *original* energy was Light - - that's the Prana! This is the energy that created our universe (e.g., the Genesis depiction) and became the 7.23 cm energy that sustains us today. It is the energy that we use to create consciousness. And the above picture says that it, too, creates the darkness - - and this means it is ultimately what's responsible for the bad-guys. Some call this original energy God, God's Light, God's Love, etc.

Thus, in spite of all the "badness", the Light Forces always win, and that includes you and me. The Prana always wins.

It was 13,000 years ago that the Ascended Masters allowed Atlantis to sink (the Great Flood). This was a concerted effort to eliminate (or at least retard) the bad-guys. The defeat of the Nazis (the Bad-Guys) in World War II was another such effort. It worked briefly. However, by 9/11 the bad-guys once again had a stranglehold on humanity.

Meanwhile, 2012 was fast approaching. This duality consciousness experiment needed to be concluded. Such experiments encourage growth.

Because "2012" could not wait any longer, the Good-Guys finally intervened, and here we are. The experiment is coming to a rapid conclusion.

Scenario B is definitely the direction we are going. Real-time intervention by the Ascended Masters is occurring as I write this. No major catastrophes have occurred. None will. Nuclear war will not happen. Things will simply get better and better as times goes by. Miracles, such as the Aspen Event (Chapter 16), will continue. Such is the case with the Pacific Ocean. It is being kept clean of radiation. These are real events that have happened, not prophecy. We are in the midst of this transition.

Our job is to continue the effort to promote this wonderful transition. This is an exciting time of change. It seems surreal, and it is, but it is also very real. Everyone needs to wake up.

Please help in getting the word out. The sooner everyone becomes aware, the sooner we progress into the 5th dimension, and the sooner Mother Earth becomes the beautiful planet we envision.

When people hear this information for the first time, their first reaction is understandably barriers of denial and resistance. That's because everything they thought they knew is probably wrong. As they hear more and more from family members and other sources, they begin to take notice and become aware.

With that awareness comes the realization of how much we have been mind-controlled by the bad-guys. With that comes the awareness of the fear that needs to be let go. With that awareness, the myths and legends of our many religious belief systems will be challenged with reconciliation.

With that awareness comes the realization that we need to wake up and get aligned. We need to visualize our future and the beautiful Earth. Just like the girl who made the thousand rosebuds open, we will be the ones making these changes happen. We will be the ones creating these apparent miracles. To do so, we have to act and behave as if they have already happened. This is faith with clear goals and unity consciousness at work.

19.2 Real-Time Resources for More Info

Here are some resources for further supporting information and real-time updates:

--Getting Aligned For The Planetary Transformation:

This book is an excellent first step for introducing people to what's going on. It explains why things have happened and why things are happening the way they are. The Sacred Geometry approach is neutral and rewarding in and of itself, and is suitable for both males and females. The book also explains what the everyday person can do to get aligned with the 2012 process so that they are not left behind.

--ThePlanetDailyNews.com:

This is the website associated with our efforts. Its mission is to provide tools, articles, books, etc., to assist you in spreading the awareness and getting more comfortable with it. As a newspaper, it also provides articles showing miracles and events - - reflecting that things are really happening.

--YouTube Channel - The Positive Side of 2012:

This contains our own videos as well as links to others, and promotes the same agenda.

--GettingAligned.com:

This is the website for this book, and it's directly linked with ThePlanetDailyNews.com.

--LiveTheFutureNow.com:

This is the website for Gordon Asher Davidson's book "The Transfiguration of Our World". This is Scenario B. Please sign up for his newsletter, as this will provide up-to-the-minute reports on what the Ascended Masters are up to and the actual improvements being implemented.

--Drunvalo.net:

This is Drunvalo's site for learning the meditation techniques for going into the Heart and beyond.

This is an exciting time for all of us. Spreading the word requires energy. Getting Aligned (unity consciousness, etc.) requires energy. So please put in the required effort.

Donations:

You can also make donations directly to ThePlanetDailyNews.com as well as our YouTube channel The Positive Side of 2012. This allows us to reach even more people and provide better and better service.

I'd like to end with one final video. This is a radio interview a couple of years ago with Drunvalo. He did not know what to expect, so he just started talking. It turned out to be, in my opinion, a beautiful piece of work. See [Link 1601].

Thank You !!
Tom Price

Appendix

- References & Links -

Resources for More Info

Here are some resources for further supporting information and real-time updates:

--Getting Aligned For The Planetary Transformation:

This book is an excellent first step for4 introducing people to what's going on. It explains why things have happened and why things are happening the way they are. The Sacred Geometry approach is neutral and rewarding in and of itself, and is suitable for both males and females. The book also explains what the everyday person can do to get aligned with the 2012 process so that they are not left behind.

--ThePlanetDailyNews.com:

This is the website associated with our efforts. Its mission is to provide tools, articles, books, etc., to assist you in spreading the awareness and getting more comfortable with it. As a newspaper, it also provides articles showing miracles and events ˗ ˗ reflecting that things are really happening.

--Channel - The Positive Side of 2012:

This YouTube channel contains our own videos as well as links to others, and promotes the same agenda. Reviewing the videos in order provide hard evidence that "The chaos in the world in unfolding according to a much higher plan". This implies that there is intervention by the higher-up in the universe, and there is.

--GettingAligned.com:

This is the website for this book, and it's directly linked with ThePlanetDailyNews.com. Other books are listed as well a store for purchasing other items.

--LiveTheFuturenow.com

This is the website for Gordon Asher Davidson's book "The Transfiguration of Our World". This is Scenario B in Chapter 18 (The Future). Please sign up for his Galactic News, as this will provide up-to-the-minute reports on what the Ascended Masters are up to and the actual improvements being implemented.

--Drunvalo.net

This is Drunvalo Melchizedek's site for learning the meditation techniques for going into the Heart and beyond.

———————

This is an exciting time for all of us. Spreading the word requires energy. Getting Aligned (unity consciousness, etc.) requires energy. So please put in the required effort.

--Donations

You can also make donations directly to ThePlanetDailyNews.com as well as our YouTube channel The Positive Side of 2012. This allows us to reach even more people and provide better and better service.

20.2 Books (9 Count)

[1]   The Ancient Secrets of the Flower of Life, Volume 1 & 2, by Drunvalo Melchizedek, Light Technology Publishing, 2000.

[2]   The Quest by Tom Brown, Jr., The Berkley Publishing Group, 1991.

[3]   Living in the Heart by Drunvalo Melchizedek, Light Technology Publishing, 2003.

[4]   The Emerald Tablets by Doreal, published by Source Book, Inc., 2006.

[5]   The Transfiguration of Our World by Gordon Asher Davidson, Golden Firebird Press, 2015.

[6]   A Universe from Nothing by Lawrence Krauss, published by Free Press, 2012.

[7]   Death on Mars: The Discovery of a Planetary Nuclear Massacre by John E. Brandenburg, Adventures Unlimited Press, 2015.

[8]   The Code - Ancient Advanced Technology and the Global Earth Matrix - Carl Munck's Complete 4 Part DVD Series

[9]   There is a River (The Story of Edgar Cayce) by Thomas Sugrue, published by Penguin Group, 2015.

20.3 *Links & Video Links (40 Count)*

101)   Drunvalo Melchizedek: Birth of a New Humanity (2 hrs). Full-length documentary of the Great Fall, the Hebrew, the bad-guys, and Tree of Life on Atlantis; The Big Fix and corresponding ceremonies on the Birth of the new Grid.

https://youtu.be/-rkqA1eaFB8

102)   The Maya of Eternal Time 2012 and Beyond (Full Documentary). This is the full length documentary (2 hrs) of the Precession of the Equinox, and the responsibility of humankind to keep up with those changes.

http://tinyurl.com/z3rx8vc

- - - Consciousness Grid - - -

401)   David Wilcock, Awake and Aware Conference, Los Angeles, Sept 2009. Technical presentation on the grid, spontaneous life generation, energy of universe and how it affects us.

https://youtu.be/scym0WH3Jww

- - - Lucifer - - -

501)   Pope John Paul II rejects reality of a literal hell. Pope and Billy Graham both reject the idea of a physical hell.

http://tinyurl.com/o7hwo

- - - History of the Earth - - -

601)   Michael Tellinger : Ancient technology and the Ubuntu movement. Physical structures in South Africa reveal the harnessing of free energy to transport gold off the planet. Four miles underground are precision drilled, ancient mine shafts.

http://tinyurl.com/p5kq9ue

- - - The Big Fix - - -

801)   The Planetary Grids Anatomy Of Gaia (Earth) by Abjini Arraíz. Placing Crystals Around the Earth   An example of a calling to do so.

http://tinyurl.com/h4hpskk

802)   Birth of a New Humanity (3/9) - - Carl Munck Code. This is Drunvalo's segment from Birth of a New Humanity. It shows that each ancient structure around the world reveals direct clues, in plain sight, which states their GPS position. Gives references for the actual Carl Munck website.

http://tinyurl.com/hgro9pd

- - - The Wise Men (and Women) - - -

1101)   The Essenes - Edgar Cayce on the Life & Times of Jesus, by McMillinMedia

http://tinyurl.com/gvqmcox

1102)   Preparation (for the coming of the Messiah), by McMillinMedia

http://www.mcmillinmedia.com/store/

1103)   Introduction: Edgar Cayce on the Life & Times of Jesus. Displays the Past Lives of Jesus, reading the Akashic Records, by McMillinMedia

http://tinyurl.com/zxrorv4

1104)   The Nativity - Edgar Cayce on the Life & Times of Jesus, by McMillinMedia

http://www.mcmillinmedia.com/store/

1105)   Herod's Massacre - Edgar Cayce on the Life & Times of Jesus, by McMillinMedia

http://tinyurl.com/zmx8ju2

- - - Jesus - - -

1201)   Flight To Egypt - Edgar Cayce on the Life & Times of Jesus, by McMillinMedia

http://www.mcmillinmedia.com/store/

1202)   *Travels Abroad - Edgar Cayce on the Life & Times of Jesus. His travels to India and Persia, by McMillinMedia*

http://www.mcmillinmedia.com/store/

1203)   *The Missing Years - Edgar Cayce on the Life & Times of Jesus. Travels to Egypt and with John, by McMillinMedia*

http://tinyurl.com/zdbmyp9

1204)   *Ministry, Part 1 - Edgar Cayce on the Life & Times of Jesus, by McMillinMedia*

http://www.mcmillinmedia.com/store/

1205)   *Ministry, Part 2 - Edgar Cayce on the Life & Times of Jesus, by McMillinMedia*

http://www.mcmillinmedia.com/store/

1206)   *Children Opening Rosebuds. The 'Super Psychics' of China, have been recognised and nurtured by their Government for the last 25 years*

http://tinyurl.com/h3g4epk

1207)   *The Indigo Evolution Full Length Documentary Indigo children*

https://youtu.be/62_qceaH3UE

1208)   *The Last Week - Edgar Cayce on the Life & Times of Jesus*

http://tinyurl.com/gnl5gvj

1209)   *Resurrection & Ascension - Edgar Cayce on the Life & Times of Jesus*

http://www.mcmillinmedia.com/store/

· · · The Melchizedek Files · · ·

1201) *The Melchizedek Priesthood 1 of 3, by Charles Taze Russell*

http://tinyurl.com/hsr4dhp

1302) Conclusion - Edgar Cayce on the Life & Times of Jesus. General discussion talking about metaphysical versus Bible. Jesus came to Geneva

http://www.mcmillinmedia.com/store/

· · · Loose Ends · · ·

1401) *The Real Philadelphia Experiment. Documentary making a ship disappear in WW II. At the end is Al Belick, who was one of the two soldiers who jumped ship during the experiment and wound up traveling in time (from 1942 to 1985, and back). Montauk experiment is more time machine work thereafter.*

http://tinyurl.com/ze3qqln

1402) *Philadelphia & Montauk Project Survivor, a True Time Traveler. Al Belick introducing his CD of the Philadelphia, Montauk projects, etc.*

http://tinyurl.com/gt8kkw6

1403) *Dr Judy Wood : Evidence of breakthrough energy technology on 9/11. The Trade Center towers turned to dust. This is a presentation of the scientific evidence.*

http://tinyurl.com/o4et3dr

1404) *Full Documentary – Khazars: History of the Bad Guys maniputlation of the Hebrew Faith to satisy their own greed and means.*

http://tinyurl.com/jfafojt

1405) *The Truth - Rothschild & the Khazar History - Documentary*
http://tinyurl.com/z39g5tj

- - - Getting Aligned - - -

1501) *Drunvalo Melchizedek interview in Yaxha Guatemala (2007).
The Leader of the Mayans wants Drunvalo & Co. to participate in
ceremony, and share their ancient secrets with the world for the first
time in 500 years. Talks about a 10 year window to fulfill the prophecy
and other due diligence.*

http://tinyurl.com/hsdhq8m

1503) *Unity Breath Audio Meditation by Drunvalo. This guided
meditation brings you, Mother Earth, and Father Sky together, just as
the ancients do.*

http://tinyurl.com/glgwgcz

1504) *Entering into the Sacred Space within the Heart - Male Way.
This is a meditation to bring you into the Sacred Space of the Heart. Do
the Unity Breath above first to establish the proper vibration, and then
do this immediately after. While you still have that vibration.*

http://tinyurl.com/gpy8e2y

1505) *Entering into the Sacred Space within the Heart - Female Way.
This is a meditation to bring you into the Sacred Space of the Heart. Do
the Unity Breath above first to establish the proper vibration, and then
do this immediately after. While you still have that vibration.*

http://tinyurl.com/hxetc9z

- - - The Awakening - - -

1601) *Radio Show with Drunvalo. Nice radio program talking about
Mother Earth, Going into the Heart, Where we are, and what the
Mayans want. A great summary.*

http://tinyurl.com/njtvdhz

1602) *A Conversation with Drunvalo Melchizedek and Adam Trombly
Fukushima Rain in Aspen Colorado Aug 2013*

http://tinyurl.com/jhk645s

1603) *Kiesha Crowler 2015. Keisha has communicated with Mother
Earth all her life. This talk emphasizes using crystals to heal the Earth
of Fukushima radiation*

http://tinyurl.com/hbcsbum

1604) Drunvalo Melchizedek - (Children Born After 1972, Part 13) by Pablo Arellano

http://tinyurl.com/hmm3c9e

1605) *Linda Madini – Raising our Vibrational Frequency. Intuitiveflow.com*

http://tinyurl.com/gue98sq

1606) *Phi Ratio from Circle & EQ Triangle,* http://www.cut-the-knot.org/do_you_know/Buratino2.shtml

http://tinyurl.com/j3hwrab

- - - The Future - - -

1801) *(Part 3/3) Importance of being in our Heart NOW! Excellent Interview explaining the Now.*

http://tinyurl.com/jxrzyyy

1802) *Gordon Asher Davidson: An Update on the Intervention by Ascened Masters.*

http://tinyurl.com/gmkahnn

Moving Around

- Figures & Verses -

20.4 List of Figures

Scroll the Table of Contents (for the section numbers listed below) to locate the picture.

The most common pictures are also bookmarked for your convenience (go to your Bookmarks). These are shown below with [brackets].

20.5 List of Bible Verses, etc.

Scroll the Table of Contents (for the section numbers listed below) to locate the verse.

Keep Updated
On This "2012 Transition"

Visit our **Web Page**

ThePlanetDailyNews.com

for the most immediate updates and products to help you.

Subscribe to **YouTube Channel**

The Positive Side of 2012

For much deeper insights and lessons on 2012
This is a great place to send your friends

FACEBOOK & TWITTER.

Are other avenues to be reminded of new videos
The latest info & up-to-minute news & events
Facebook.com/PositiveSideof2012
Twitter.com/ThePlanetDailyN

40432507R00131

Made in the USA
Middletown, DE
12 February 2017